23778

DS
557
.A69
D8

Duncan
        The new legions

THE NEW LEGIONS

THE NEW LEGIONS

by Donald Duncan

 RANDOM HOUSE • New York

TO LARRY AND MY OTHER FRIENDS—

WHO ARE ANOTHER KIND OF LEGION

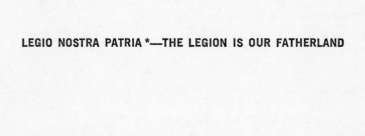

LEGIO NOSTRA PATRIA *—THE LEGION IS OUR FATHERLAND

* Unofficial motto of the French Foreign Legion

"*To fight you must be brutal and ruthless and the spirit of ruthless brutality will enter into the very fibre of our national life, infecting Congress, the courts, the policeman on the beat, the man in the street. . . .*"

WOODROW WILSON

EARLY LIGHT makes its way past dark buildings to fall on a street deserted except for the group gathered in front of a sooty-bricked office. Most are young men carrying small new handbags, combination farewell and Christmas presents. They are dessed in Levis and slacks, "Ike" jackets and sport coats, open sport shirts and white shirts with ties, loafers, oxfords, sneakers. Fat, short, tall, skinny, teen-ager, young adult, school dropout, college graduate; as many different personalities as there are bodies. All are here because of forces as far beyond their control as the sun rising over the unfolding scene.

Each young man is an island, because he is completely surrounded by parents, younger brothers, a girl friend, a wife, or because he is surrounded by the absence of these well-wishers. The islands are strangers who have not yet found a common sea. Those without company puff on cigarettes and study the dimpled cement to avoid the embarrassment of witnessing an emotional scene. Those with company engage in forced laugher and conversation to avoid an emotional scene. Younger brothers look with envious eyes at the young men who attempt in turn to be worthy of the envy with an air of nonchalance and an "I do things like this every day" that doesn't quite come off. Girl friends project mixed images of bravery and tragedy, wives display worry and pride, fathers gruffly attempt to make last-minute infusions of masculinity, mothers dab at moist eyes, reluctant to release their boys to an alien masculine world. Feet shuffle, shoulders shrug in jackets, a cigarette is flipped toward two buses parked at the curb which give ominous witness to the tableau.

"Mom, I can't carry all that. They'll feed me . . ."

". . . just as soon as I get there . . ."

"We'll get married as soon as I get back, Ruth . . ."

". . . won't be cold. We're going south."

"Give 'em hell, Son . . ."

Well-wisher or young man with a handbag, stranger, individual—all have one other thing in common beyond having no control over the powers that have brought them to this place on this day. Whether they would prolong the drama or wish it were finished, all are uncomfortable, self-conscious.

With a mixed sense of reluctance and relief all turn from their thoughts and conversation when the door of the red building opens. A rumpled little man in a blue suit, looking like a male Betty Crocker, adjusts his wire glasses, rustles his sheaf of papers, and clears his throat officiously. This insignificant little man at this moment at this place is the personification of direction emanating from uncontrollable forces.

"Gentlemen, please give me your attention. When I call your name, answer with your first name and middle initial and then load on the first bus . . . Abels . . . Acheson . . . Albo . . . Bradshaw . . . Brite . . . Calvert . . . Campi . . . Damonte . . . DiMarco . . . Duncan . . ."

"Donald W.," I shout and move to the bus.

Induction Day. Rochester, New York. December 27, 1954.

From Local Board 73 in Rochester to the Armory in Buffalo with a busload of strangers and stranger thoughts. (Why is it called Selective Service instead of Selecting Service?) In Buffalo the roster with the rumpled blue suit is replaced by a roster with a carefully pressed olive-drab suit featuring two chevrons on each sleeve. Other strangers had preceded us.

"Gentlemen, when I call your name, line up on the painted line. Aaron . . . Abels . . ."

"Gentlemen, turn to your right and follow . . ."

"Do not touch the papers on the table. On the wall is a blow-up of the form in front of you. I will explain how to fill in the blocks. Don't get ahead. In block number one, where it says 'Date,' print today's date. The date today is two seven, twenty-seven December one niner five four. In block number two print your last name first, then your first . . ." Monotone.

Lesson number one—it is no longer December 27, it is 27 December.

"Gentlemen, turn to your left and follow . . ."

"Take off all your clothes except your shorts. Take your billfolds with you." Monotone from Four Stripes. Another roster call.

"When you get a bottle, go to the latrine on your left, fill it, and return to the same place in line. Stay there . . ."

Bumps, shouts, curses, and the ammonia smell of spilled urine. Obediently back in line clutching a warm bottle—eyes averted. Tablets dissolved, specimens examined, bottles emptied, more curses, back in line.

"Gentlemen, put your feet on the line. Place your billfolds by the right foot. The doctors will come by . . ."

White coats . . . stethoscopes . . . tapping fingers . . . "say 'ahhh' " . . . lights in eyes . . . nervous sweat . . .

"Gentlemen, drop your shorts."

Rubber-gloved doctors pass down the rows of naked men. "Milk it down. Turn your head. Cough . . . again . . ."

"When the doctor walks behind you, bend forward at the waist, reach behind you with both hands and spread your cheeks." Monotone with a leer. Mass obscenity.

The beginning of initiation into the totally organized life. Stripped of clothing and civilian identity. Poked, prodded, and impersonally examined by the dead-eyed, cold-fingered medics. We shuffled from line to line in response to an unholy design. There was little talking or laughter among the naked. The conversation of the others —the ones in clothes—was conducted as if we didn't exist or couldn't hear. We stared at the floor as dumbly as tongueless inmates in an asylum. Fat, short, tall, skinny, teen-ager, young adult, school dropout, college graduate. All entered the building as individuals. There are now as many bodies as there were individuals, getting ready to take the next step toward becoming the lowest common denominator—Recruit, U.S. Army.

Clothes are retrieved. More lines. More herding. More rosters. Back to the large examining room. A wooden stand holding the American flag has been placed at the front of the room.

"In a moment an officer will swear you in as members of the United States Army. Draftees who are not citizens of the United States of America are not required to take the oath of enlistment. Those choosing not to take the oath will be escorted by personnel from the Immigration Service to the nearest port-of-entry."

Monotone with six stripes is replaced by monotone with silver bars on his shoulders. "Those *wishing* to enlist in the United States Army will so signify by taking one step forward . . ."

Draftees forced to answer the call or risk imprisonment—many see the contradiction but take the step toward the flag, symbol of the United States and its Constitution.

"Stand at attention and raise your right hand. Repeat after me . . ."

So much for involuntary servitude and the Thirteenth Amendment. The room is silent witness to the second obscenity of the day.

Soldiers. Privates. An appropriate title, no doubt earned by having the same so thoroughly and publicly inspected.

Herding, rosters, and waiting. Men gather in groups to talk. Others crowd around Five Stripes and inquire about the future. A few wander from group to group. All are earnest. Most show anxiety for the real or imagined trials of the future. To some it is an adventure, to others an ordeal. They would rather be home, but now committed they want to get on with it.

Stacks of paper emanating from some mysterious source pass back and forth in the care of uniformed men with spit-polished shoes and short haircuts. What the papers are and where they are going remain a mystery, but we instinctively feel they contain plans for our lives beyond our control.

A pile of mimeographed paper terminates its journey at Five Stripes' table-throne. Conversation ends abruptly. He looks at the papers and announces that "you gentlemen" will be going to Fort Knox, Kentucky. He passes out copies of these depersonalized orders.

"Aaron . . . Acheson . . ."

Wonder what happened to Abels?

I glance at my copy: UP AR . . . fol rsg . . . sta . . . ALOC . . . BPED . . . ETS . . . EDCSA—undoubtedly a secret code to boggle the minds of enemy agents. Finally a long list of names . . . there it is . . . DUNCAN, DONALD W. E-1 (rct.) . . . US 51 337 577. It is official. I am government property and have a serial number to prove it.

It is dark when we are herded to the Pullmans waiting to take us to Fort Knox. The last we see of the building before we pass into the night is a poster depicting a helmeted soldier clutching what looks like a laundry bag to his stomach and trying to jump feet first into the room. The block letters say:

BE PROUD . . . GO AIRBORNE . . . US ARMY

"The average man's capacity for rational judgment steadily declines once he has turned over the responsibility to the 'organizer,' the responsibility for making decisions."

KARL MANNHEIM

EIGHT MEN. A small number if we get into trouble. Eight men to go into a VC area where, if J-2 intelligence is correct, eighty wouldn't help. Only stealth can protect us, and for that we are four too many. A bell rings, the chopper heaves into the air, and those on the ground disappear in a billow of dust. A slow turn to the right and we can see the other H-34 following.

I glance at Hoa, the Vietnamese lieutenant who sits beside me in the doorway, studying his map. Not a strong leader, but he does know the jungle; more important, he knows his weakness and allows Boxie,* medic-turned-team sergeant, to do the leading. As usual, Boxie is within arm's reach behind me. Sitting on the canvas seat next to the door is Grady, my American assistant. Like the rest of us, he has his soft camouflage hat tucked in the front of his shirt, a precaution against loss in the prop blast at "unassing" time. First time out with Grady—short and a little paunchy, the light reflecting from his forehead—who comes highly recommended. Sensing my eyes, he returns the smile with controlled nervousness.

As far forward as space will permit are the four Vietnamese who complete the team; they sit in various positions, each having found his own way to ease his pack's

* Americanization of *Bac-si*—Vietnamese for "doctor."

weight. I know the radio operator and the little Montagnard who acts as our point man; like Boxie, he has been with me on many such trips. The other two are last-minute replacements, but at least they know enough to stay forward in the cabin, despite discomfort, in order to keep the weight under the main rotor. I give them all a "Gay Adventurer" smile and the "thumbs up" with my right hand; both are returned, and Boxie pats my shoulder, his gold teeth gleaming.

I lean back on my pack to ease the weight, letting my legs dangle outside. At this altitude the air is cold. Under the drone of the motor we retreat into our thoughts. Trouble? Going into a VC area to verify their strength and location is a poor way to avoid it. If past performance is any indication, we'll get the answers when the shooting starts. How many such trips does this one make? A mental shrug, and then I complete an inventory of the pack on my back. Without moving, I rehearse extracting magazines from my AR-15 * and slapping new ones home without looking. I think back over our hurried briefing.

The bell rings—the pilots informing us we are passing our operational area. I heave to a sitting position to look at the terrain which will be our home for the next four or five days. There isn't much to see—two bare ridgelines, almost parallel, sticking up through the jungle canopy. Running north to south, a little closer together at the southern end, they mark the boundaries of the six-mile valley we must investigate. I shiver involuntarily. Thousands of miles flown over similar canopies, but it always looks ominously different when you know that soon you'll be walking beneath it. What do those treetops

---

* Colt Armelite AR-15 or U.S. Rifle M-16.

hide? How many unfriendly eyes watch us pass? What is responsible for those wisps of smoke at the southern end? From two thousand feet up it is impossible to make out details in the black-greenness below.

We all lean back. It will be at least thirty minutes before we go in. The pilot will take us out of the area until the light fades; we will return from a different angle. I pull out my map and stare at it for the umpteenth time since our briefing, trying to memorize every detail and fix each feature on the back of my eyeballs. Something on the map doesn't quite jibe with what I've just seen below. I shrug—I guess it never really does. The crew chief taps me on the shoulder and points out the door to a village half in flames—natural disaster or VC attack . . .

The light is fading fast; it won't be long now. As if to agree, the chopper banks right and starts losing altitude. Each man looks to his weapon. Left hands tap magazines and slip foward to grasp hand guards . . . right hands retract operating slides . . . heads bend over to make sure a round is feeding into the chamber . . . slides and bolts ram home . . . selectors put on "safe" . . . another reassuring tap on the magazine to make sure it is secure . . . a final fiddling with harness webbing and pack straps . . . then tenseness. For the first time I notice that my clothes are sweat-damp, and at two thousand feet it can't be the heat; I smell sour and hope nobody has noticed. At treetop level now, the air is much warmer, and I raise my feet instinctively as a tree rushes by at eighty knots.

Straight down is the jungle's black mass. My stomach tightens. Will this be the time we land in the middle of them? Leaning forward, I turn my face to the wind, straining futilely to see our destination. I'm not disappointed when I can't locate it. It will be small and unlike landing zones favored by U.S. pilots for assault landings. The VC won't expect a chopper, especially at this time of night. In trail, silhouetted against the remaining light, is the H-34 carrying Manny's team to another area.

A loss of air speed throws our weight forward and the chopper starts vibrating violently; we're going straight down. Long grass, flattened by the prop blast, suddenly appears. Boxie's hand is on my shoulder. Safety off. Hoa and I heave ourselves from the doorway. Damn: water under the grass—so much for dry socks and foot powder. We lurch forward, water and grass grabbing at our legs while the rotors' blast tries to buckle our knees. The pilot isn't really sitting down in this muck: the hydraulic struts are still extended and the motor is at full rpm. We stop to let Boxie and the point man pass between us. Hoa looks to the black jungle a few yards ahead while I turn to face the chopper. Grady will be the last man out. As I turn I glimpse the blue exhaust flame of Manny's H-34 passing close overhead; hopefully, his noise will prevent anyone nearby from knowing one machine has landed. As Grady starts from the door I give the "thumbs up," and before his feet touch down the chopper leaps straight into the air and falls in line behind its partner, the change in pitch knocking down the man in front of Grady. The chopper hasn't been down four seconds and within a couple more we are together at the treeline.

Holding on to each other's pack, we move a short distance into the trees and stop. The blackness is complete; so is the silence roaring in our straining ears. The hand holding on to a buddy's pack is as invisible as the pack and the man carrying it. Hearts beat fast. This is the critical period. It will be at least an hour and a half before we can make radio contact, and if anything should happen now, even if base knew about it, there is damned little they could do. The advantage is all with the enemy.

Hands grope over me in a familiar ritual and find the stubble on my face. A faint click precedes the luminous glow of a compass held in Hoa's disembodied hands. The team is bunched up now, and I'm relieved to find that I'm not the only one who smells raunchy. I take out my own compass. The azimuth shown on Hoa's compass is a proposed line of march. I match it with my own to show that I understand, and then slowly turn it to indicate another direction. Over the face of the compass I pass my forefinger counterclockwise in a half circle and then let it shoot off at a right tangent into the darkness. There is a slight hesitation, and then Hoa's compass face disappears under his hand: he has accepted my suggestion. The point man, smelling of sour sweat, fish, and *nuoc-mam*,* moves to our side. Hoa repeats my performance and the point does the same with his compass. Hearing no other movement, we start off on a route which will take us in a large half circle around our landing zone. First the little Montagnard, then Boxie, Hoa, myself, the radio man, Grady, and the two replacements. We move slowly, stopping every few minutes to listen.

---

* An oily sauce made from fish in much the same manner as sauerkraut is made from cabbage. Its odor, usually very offensive to Western nostrils, is relished by the Vietnamese; as one told me, "*Nuoc-mam* smells so good that it makes the teeth ache wanting it." Although I used this pungent sauce on numerous occasions when dining with Vietnamese friends, I avoided it on these missions because its salt content creates an intolerable thirst, and because not having its odor in my head, I was able to detect VC jungle encampments from the all-pervading smell, despite my smoking habit—testimony to its strength.

Finally I hear it: running water. I move forward to investigate. Great—too small to be a drinking and washing stream for an enemy encampment, it will guide us uphill and spare us from having to crash through the thick undergrowth. For feet already wet from the landing, walking the stream will be no hardship.

For thirty minutes we move up the stream and then cut off left, back into the thick brush. Thirty meters in we stop to rest and form a crude circle. In a few minutes I feel a tap on my arm: Boxie, whispering in my ear— part bad French, part worse English, the rest Vietnamese. One of the new men has lost his map, on which, if he followed usual practice, he has marked the limits of our area, the LZ,* and probable route of march. The man doesn't know where or when it was lost—perhaps when he fell as the chopper took off, perhaps later. Practice makes it easy not to get angry at what could well mean disaster. Boxie asks if we should go back and look for it, and I can feel his relief when I say no, it would be impossible to find at night. Hoa wants to know what we should do; he wants me to say that the mission is compromised and we should ask for exfiltration.† Before I can answer, we hear a distant shot. As if on signal compasses open immediately. "Charlie" has made our decision for us. The sound came from the direction of the LZ.

We move on for about twenty minutes, then walk in a wide circle and stop. We will stay here for the night. Again we form a rough circle. I pair up with Grady, since I want to be close in case he snores—a sound that nothing in the jungle can duplicate. Boxie makes sure each man knows the location of the other seven, and reminds

* Landing zone.
† Armyese for infiltrating from an area, as opposed to infiltrating into an area.

each of the rendezvous point should we get separated in a fight during the night.

I take off my pack, lift out the ground sheet and HT-1 radio. Crawling under the ground sheet, I draft a message with the aid of a red-filtered penlight. That done, I take off my boots and wring the excess water from my socks; I'll walk them dry in the morning. Surprisingly, there are very few leeches on me. After an application of mosquito repellant, which also wards off leeches, I slip on a black nylon sailing parka. In a few minutes the radio contact plane will be nearby.

Sporadic firing. Everyone sits up. Compasses open. Sure enough the noise is from the LZ. (It is a favorite VC trick to fire randomly, hoping it will be returned and reveal an enemy's position.) Have they found the map? If not, they can only guess if someone is in the area. Chances are they have. In any event, the VC aren't going far at night unless they travel trails and paths, and we aren't close to either. If they have the map, they know we're here, and the hunters will become the hunted in the morning.

I can hear the distant drone of a C-47, our contact. Back under the ground sheet I affix the earplug attached to the radio, turn the set on, and push the transmit button three times. I'm not going to talk until I know there is contact. Then, with a loudness that makes me flinch, "Sunflower One, this is Gilded Cage. Do you have traffic? Over."

I cup my hands around the mouthpiece and whisper hoarsely, "This is Sunflower. Affirmative. Do you read me? Over."

"This is Gilded Cage. Read you five-by.* Send your message. Over."

* Five-by-five—loud and clear.

Enunciating carefully, I transmit our location and possible destination, using Q and Zs with letter transposition.* Cryptically, slowly, I explain about the missing map and enemy firing. We'll continue the mission. I send the message without a break in transmission—bad procedure but presently expedient. "How copy? Over."

"This is Gilded Cage. I read back . . ."

Miraculous: right the first time.

"If message correct and you have no further transmission, acknowledge by pushing button twice . . . Roger. Understand no further transmission. Out."

After stowing the radio and redoing the pack, I lie on my back and use it as a pillow. Weapon across my stomach, right hand on the pistol grip, I review the few hours since our landing. That damned map—what could be marked on it? Too bad about the LZ—one less place to use for our exfiltration in the event of trouble. The map. I think of markings delineating our operational boundaries and . . . map . . . boundaries . . . Christ! I almost sit up. That's what doesn't jibe. From the air the ridges marking our boundaries narrow only slightly. The contour lines on the map, however, crowd and almost overlap from each ridge to a small stream between the two. The trees must hide the slopes. Three miles between the rows where we are, the valley must come to a V in the south. We have to go south and there won't be any place to land a helicopter until we're a couple of miles southwest of the gap. If "Charlie" has the map and knows we are here, it will be a trap.

This is what has been bothering me since the briefing, what I couldn't see on our recon flight this morning: a

---

* Simple brevity code normally used with Morse code transmission; letter transposition—a simple code form used to send map coordinates verbally.

box with no way out. It's going to take some very accurate and careful navigation to squeeze through. Expecting a trap will make it less of one, and we'll have to figure where it may be sprung. As soon as there is enough light I'll have to study that map. A final careful listen, and I start to doze. Changes in the predawn jungle noises will wake me, as will Grady's snoring, if he can sleep.

● ● ●

My eyes are open. Blackness. Grady's breathing tells me he isn't asleep. I listen—a frond falling, a nut bouncing downward, the night animals are quiet, and within thirty minutes the day birds will start chattering. Without moving my buttocks, I come to a cross-legged sitting position. Reaching behind me I carefully move my pack to the front. Wet to the knees from walking in water, I am equally wet to the neck from the previous night's exertions. I remove the nylon parka and shiver at the sudden loss of body heat; my shirt has become a cold compress. Rolled in a tight wad, the parka goes into the pack. Easing the ground sheet from under me, I wrap it around the small radio and in it goes.

The pack secure, I touch Grady's shoulder: he is shivering from the damp cold, and touches my hand to signify understanding. Boxie will see that the others are stirring. From a side pocket on the pack I take a small plastic envelope of precooked rice to which I add dried pineapple chunks and some sugar, then water from my plastic canteen, using the middle finger of my left hand to tell when the envelope is full. Returning the canteen to its pouch, I fold and twist the envelope closed, secure it with a rubber band, and stow it in the pocket. The first birds are making themselves known. Still no light, but the blackness is thinner now and I can see Grady's outline. I slowly pass a dry toothbrush over my teeth behind closed lips, and restrain the exquisite desire to clear my throat—a forbidden luxury and self-imposed torture for a heavy smoker. Two salt tablets and a swig of water. With a piece of hard candy in my mouth, I refasten the pocket and slip the pack around to my rear. Leaning back, I wiggle my arms through the shoulder straps and rest on the pack. Individual trees can be distinguished—morning twilight. As soon as I can see Boxie, it will be time to move.

First to a sitting position, then rock forward onto the knees, left knee up, foot on the ground. Eight men rise to a standing position. Everyone listens. The birds and squirrels are now in full chorus. I turn outward from the circle as do the others, a concession to modesty while urinating. When I turn back, Boxie, Hoa, and the point man are looking at me. I point at the jungle—southeast. Boxie and Hoa frown. The nod is given to the point. They know I'll explain later. Distance between each man is determined by the available light. Vines grab, thorns rake against the hand holding the weapon, another scratches an ear, a broad leaf slaps my face. No hacking here. Patience. No yanking when a vine snaps and holds. Reach around with the free hand and loosen it or wait until the man behind comes up and let him do it. As always, I am amazed that we walked through the same mess in pitch dark without breaking a leg or waking the entire jungle.

We proceed slowly, the distance between men increasing with the light. Black is replaced by green, vision is restricted to a few yards. Sweating again, the cold forgotten, we move for ninety minutes, pausing only to listen to the jungle sounds. There is a conscious effort not to lose tempers at the thousand-fingered brush, vines, and thorns impeding progress and tearing at skin and clothing.

We stop. Boxie, the point man, and the two trail men fade into the undergrowth. The rest get down on one knee to wait, weapons at the ready. Within ten minutes Boxie returns and gives the "thumbs up," meaning that there are no paths or trails in the immediate area, no unusual noises, and the three men have been posted as lookouts.

Boxie and Grady help the radio operator string the long-wire antenna for the large radio, while Hoa and I huddle and discuss the situation in whispers. The map has confirmed my fears of the night before. Using the map and sticks on the ground, I trace our path around the LZ, and our turns east and up the small stream and northeast to our night camp; on the map I point to what I judge is our present location. Hoa's frown indicates his disagreement, and with the long pointed nail on his left little finger he indicates his choice. Neither of us is upset for with no prominent terrain features we could both be wrong. I explain about the map, no LZs, the narrow passage at the south end of the valley, and possible places for an ambush. He understands most of this already, so despite language difficulties it doesn't take long. I suggest a route that will take us diagonally back and forth across the valley. We agree that the most likely ambush sites will be along two stream branches which run across the valley into a larger stream running south. The western side of the gap looks like our best bet for sneaking through.

Hoa goes to the radio to draft a message with Boxie.

The operator will use CW,* because it is quiet and will enable him to send a more detailed account than I could using voice last night. Grady and I fish the rice envelopes from each other's packs. Removing the band from the top, I pinch off mouthfuls of the now thick, glutinous mass and milk them up the bag to my mouth. A couple of mouthfuls of water and so much for breakfast.

We each light cigarettes and I repeat my whispered conversation. I don't tell Grady, as I didn't tell Hoa, that unless we can positively pinpoint our location by early afternoon, we are in serious trouble. Our one hope is to know exactly where we are at all times; an error of fifty feet in the gap will be disastrous.

Breakfast over (the Vietnamese have had dried shrimp soaked in *nuoc-mam* with their rice) and the radio again on the operator's back, we prepare to resume our march.

Bang!

Spin around . . . down on one knee . . . heart pounding . . . eyes straining toward the jungle . . . ears cocked for snapping brush. Nobody returns fire: a result of training or of fear? The shot seemed close but not that close—perhaps twenty minutes on our backtrail. To confirm this, I look at the team. Each man gives a negative headshake; the bullet hasn't come close enough to anyone to make that peculiar *crack* of a near hit. A lone hunter? I would like to believe that but can't. We rise quietly and resume our march.

In spite of our caution a stick occasionally snaps, and we must remind ourselves that the sound doesn't travel

* Continuous-wave transmission; the sending of Morse Code by radio, using a telegrapher's key as opposed to voice transmission.

far and that other things in the jungle sound similar. We are making relatively good time, and the vines and scrub thorn don't seem quite so thick here. My clothes are heavy with sweat, salt burns my eyes, and as usual the humidity is a smothering blanket. Even the Vietnamese sweat visibly. Here, sweating means only a loss of body fluid. After fifty minutes we stop, staying in line, well spread out.

Two more salt tablets and a drink. Water—it could be a problem. Hoa walks back with his map; I take mine from my pants leg pocket and study it for a few minutes.

"I think we are right here," and indicate with my pen.

"No. For sure, we here." The long fingernail again— half a grid square away and further down the valley. Am I wrong or has fatigue made him overestimate distance? We must resolve this soon.

"Hoa, tell the men to use their water carefully. If VC know we are here, they will have all water guarded." Must be my day for saying unnecessary things. Hoa knows this already, and saying it won't affect water consumption. We start moving again.

Bang!

Spin . . . kneel . . . search with the eyes. Again just one shot. Again the same march distance away on our backtrail. We look at each other. No emotion shows. There is no doubt now: we are being followed; the shot is to keep those ahead posted on our progress. I grudgingly admit that it is a pretty good psychological gambit. The march is resumed.

Now we're getting into real thick stuff: dense, bushy thorn trees with branches almost to the ground join together in a tangle of vines. We duck-walk and crawl more than walk now. Damn! Even the vines have small grabbers or thorns on them. We'll do well to make fifty meters an hour through this. We are changing direction—generally southwest. Good. Boxie has turned the point. The VC won't follow us through this stuff. Having figured our line of march, "Charlie" will take an easier route, confident he'll pick us up further along.

We stop frequently. This is exhausting work. The thought crosses my mind that if this were a John Wayne movie, we could cut our way through with machetes or cane knives. It's a long way from Hollywood. Mind back on the job—that kind of musing can be dangerous. The water is taking a hell of a beating. I look at my watch: almost contact time. I close up on Hoa and point skyward. He passes the word and everyone stops in place, grateful for the break.

Hoa digs the HT-1 from my pack. I put in the earplug and turn on the set; only the rushing noise. I stretch out my legs to ease my tired knees. I can hear faint voices on the set, probably talking to Manny's team in the next area. Silence. A voice crashes in my ear: "Sunflower One, this is Gilded Cage. Over."

I press the talk button twice, slowly.

"Sunflower One, this is Gilded Cage. Do you have traffic for this station? Over."

Again I push the button twice.

"Roger, Sunflower. You acknowledge transmission but do not wish to transmit at this time. If this is a roger, repeat last signal twice. Over."

Two times . . . pause . . . twice more.

"Roger, Sunflower. Will fly unscheduled contact at one-three-zero-zero. Gilded Cage out."

Same operator. Good man—I'll have to remember to tell him so when we get back. Radio away, we move out. Ears tense but no shot. Have we gained a little on him?

We can stand once in a while. We are making a little

better time, but if the mice can, so too can the cat. I hand-signal a new course, more west than south; if they're waiting for us south, the longer we take to get there, the more fidgety the ambushers will become.

Twenty-five minutes more of stooping, bending, crawling, unhooking, disentangling. An arm wave, palm down, and each man freezes. I can't see the point man. Hoa turns to me and hand-signals a trail ahead. Turning back, he forms a V with the first two fingers of his left hand, jabs at his eyes, and then points north. I repeat the gesture to the two trail men but point south. They immediately slip away at a tangent. The rest wait— fifteen, twenty, twenty-five minutes.

We move forward with extreme care. Hoa stops in a kneeling position and I come alongside. Slowly we push aside some brush and ferns, and the trail becomes visible, double-tracked and well used. I glance upward—thick canopy, it won't be seen from the air.

Hoa steps around the bush and I follow. We cross the trail, careful to walk only on the hardpack so the distinctive rubber cleats of our jungle boots won't leave impressions. Knowing that the trail has been checked both north and south doesn't make me feel any less naked during the crossing. Boxie and the point are already across in guard positions. The others come across in pairs and we continue to move west.

Shortly before noon the land starts rising and we turn south. We are on the other side of the valley. After checking ahead and to our flanks, we stop for lunch—rice, vitamins, salt tablets, water. Crawling bugs and flying insects of every variety are around us; the hot air is heavy with moisture. From my pack I take a bundle that has had the Vietnamese curious since they first saw it—long-gaff tree climbers. I strap them on, hand my rifle to

Grady, and walk over to a likely-looking tree. Unable to see my legs in the ferns, the Vietnamese watch my movements with puzzlement. I start up the back side of the tree, not driving in the spurs but carefully placing them and letting my weight set them; it's slow but quiet. The tree is wide but the bark has deep rivulets for handholds. At seventy-five feet I finally see the ridgeline to the west, and at about eighty-five feet there is a good clear view of the dominant peaks. Straddling a limb, I take sightings with my compass on the peaks and carefully write down the figures in my notebook. I'll do the computation on the ground, for I feel too vulnerable this far from my rifle.

When I descend, Grady, Boxie, and Hoa are waiting; the two Vietnamese are grinning and can't keep from touching the climbing irons, giving the "thumbs up" and whispering "number one." Climbers back in the pack, I designate on the map the reading to each peak for Hoa. I compute the back azimuths on my map by substituting a protractor for the compass; Hoa does his own computation. I was very close, but Hoa has not lost face, for we both know that next time it could be the other way. Now, with our position pinpointed, we can accurately plot the trail we crossed and our future course. It will soon be 1300, so we quickly compose a message. The plane arrives on schedule and all information is relayed.

It has been a lengthy stop, but long ago I learned the futility of pushing during *"pak* time"—the Vietnamese siesta. By their standards we are moving early, and when Grady voices concern at the length of our stay, I remind him that those on the other side are also Vietnamese.

The single shot seems further back this time. I promise myself that some day I'll find out how they keep that distance and still know each time we start and stop. The afternoon is a repetition of the morning. Our direction changes from south to southeast and then in the midst of the worst entanglement we swing back to southwest. The inevitable single shot after each of our short breaks is uncanny and a little unnerving.

Late afternoon, the land is rising again. But instead of turning, we continue upward. We are getting into fallen trees and piles of jumbled rocks as well as the ubiquitous thorn brush and vines. It's noisy and we have to go slowly, but there shouldn't be any paths here. After getting through some exceptionally thick stuff, we halt and start making camp, more easily than last night because we can see what we are doing. I repeat my tree-climbing stunt and we are right on target. The big radio is set up and a short message giving our location sent.

We finish off our rice. Everybody shakes his canteen and listens with a frown. I'm doing a little better than Grady. I pour some of my water into the metal cup and add two bouillon cubes. Three small stones forming a V, and a good pinch of ignited C-4 *—and within seconds the broth is bubbling. I pour part of the contents of my cup into Grady's. Imagination being what it is, I can feel strength from the warm meaty drink oozing through my body.

Another shot. We look at each other. Our shadow again, but still no closer. The day sounds of the jungle are fading. A lizard's throaty screech startles everyone until the sound is catalogued.

Bahwhroom . . . crr-rump!

Artillery shells. About a quarter mile south. Everyone sits up. Two more explosions, and this time we can hear the revolving *whoosh* as the shells push through the air.

* Plastique explosive—easily ignited, it burns with an intensely hot flame, little odor, and no smoke, and it won't explode unless heat and shock are applied simultaneously.

That figures. A distant ARVN * artillery battery, not knowing we are here, is firing grid concentrations. I wonder if our friends waiting for us in that direction think we are calling the fire. Too bad we don't have that capability, but if "Charlie" thinks we do, maybe he'll be cautious.

The artillery stops. The light fades fast. On with the mosquito repellant and nylon parka. The crickets, fireflies, and mosquitoes compete for the night. Again I'm on my back, rifle across my stomach. Nothing to do until the contact plane shows up at 2200; tonight I will give them only the button signal unless something strange happens in the next couple of hours.

Another hour passes. Another shot—it seems to echo more at night but is still at the same distance. They know we've stopped but they also know they can't move in on us through the brush without giving warning.

The contact plane has left, the radio is packed. I squirm until I'm relatively comfortable. The canteen on each hip will prevent my rolling over. Time to rest and sleep. I close my eyes.

●   ●   ●

Eyes open now. The shot again. Moved around some but no closer. My mind registers the jungle noises—normal. Eyes close.

Again my eyes are open, looking into the blackness. The noises are changing. Another day. I feel rested. Except for the almost hourly rifle shot the night has been uneventful. I can tell by Grady's breathing that he isn't sleeping; so it was each time I awoke during the night.

* Army of the Republic of Viet-Nam, pronounced Arvin.

That could be trouble, because a tired man is a sloppy man, and dangerous. The preceding morning's scene is repeated—how many such mornings have there been for me? After I prepare my rice I have only a few mouthfuls of water left. Some of the team must decide on whether to fix rice or save water. Others won't have enough for the rice so the decision will be easy. It is going to be a long day.

South, then southeast, a repetition of the previous day. Vines, thorns, snag, unsnag, crawl, creep, more scratches. Careful, can't yield to the luxury of losing temper. And always that damned shot every time we start moving.

Afternoon now, and canteens are empty. Can't take salt tablets without water. Mouths are dry. It won't be long before we have leg trouble. Swing back southwest now toward the rocks and another night camp. It will be a dry night.

What is the enemy thinking? He must know we need water; hopefully, he doesn't know how badly. He knows we know we are being followed. Why aren't we moving south faster? Where will our route take us? He knows by now we are crisscrossing irregularly, so he can't pinpoint our course. He will have to spread out to cover the entire width of the valley, including the lower slopes on each side. The streams still seem to be the best places for ambush deployment. We have to cross those streams for two reasons: the flanks will be tightly secured on the lower slopes and we must get water. I wonder if the people following have radio contact with those ahead.

More clawing, cutting thorns and brush grab at tired legs as we move toward the night camp. Suddenly from far off to our right front drifts the muted sounds of a firefight. It must be on the other side of the ridge—

Manny's area. The men exchange glances. The volume of the fire says it must be a hell of a fight. Long, too: the firing continues for at least five minutes—too long not to take hits.

We are finally at an area similar to the one we holed up in last night, and we follow the same procedures; but only a few are eating. Boxie looks worried. The men are really beat. It has been hard slogging through the brush —and with the tension-producing knowledge that parting the next bush may precipitate a firefight, with no water and the subsequent weakening from dehydration, and with the fear of a worse tomorrow, they have good cause to be fatigued.

I eat the remainder of my rice with misgivings. It is moist and feels good in my mouth, but how much body fluid will it take to digest it? By CW we report the firefight. Since base knows our position, with the azimuth to the sound they can figure the line and see if the other team is in trouble. Tonight is a carbon copy of last night —and always that damned single shot.

● ● ●

Time to move on. I'm worried about Grady—he didn't sleep much again last night. No water to drink, no food to prepare; we are ready in record time today. We move southeast again, but more slowly than usual. Surely those following us see the pattern. I hope so. This course will bring us to the first stream at the eastern side of the ever narrowing valley. At what would normally be our breakfast break, I explain a plan I thought of while waiting for the contact plane, sketching with a stick on the ground as I talk. We keep this course until we hit the hidden north-south trail again. While six of us secure a portion of the trail, two men walk across, back up, walk across again, break a few twigs leading into the brush on the other side, and then again back up. One man with combat boots, the other with jungle boots, so the prints will show. Sure, I know it's an old trick—maybe that's why it will work.

We regroup and turn back southwest, just enough so that we don't bump into our friends tailing us. As soon as we are about halfway between the stream junction and the western wall we move straight south, fast, until we reach the river. I am counting on the belief that if the enemy has been in position two days, he will be restless, and since we have been moving so slowly, he won't expect us this early or at that place. We will have to wait until we get to the river or stream to decide how to cross.

With the first part of the plan behind us, we are moving southwest, even faster than we'd hoped. We have our compasses out and are pacing—no time for error now. Boxie looks back, Hoa gives the nod, the point turns south. We grip our weapons a little tighter.

It's getting a little thicker now but the ground is still level. The speed is telling on us all. I notice that I'm no longer sweating; Grady's clothes are dry and his shirt shows white salt stains. The Vietnamese, especially the radio operator, appear to be getting wobbly-kneed; my leg muscles are tired and close to cramping.

The halt sign from the point. Boxie comes back. We are close to the stream. Hoa, Boxie, and I go forward. The previously flat ground drops away suddenly through the brush and ferns, and although we can't see or hear the water, we know it's there. Without signal the men start taking seats and making themselves comfortable. Good team: men of lesser training in dire need of water would have moved straight to the stream. I had seen it happen with the Strike Force * in Tay Ninh.

Five minutes, ten, fift . . . to our left front. Some-one chopping. Then a voice, and another answers. The sharp crack of a large stick breaking. A man calls out. The sound of a sharp rebuke from another. They're there, waiting. Hoa, finger to his lips, motions and we start moving down the hill an inch at a time. Look . . . pick a spot . . . move a foot to the spot . . . repeat . . . move the other foot . . . careful lest the weapon knock on wood or rock. Skin is tight waiting for the bullets of a hidden machine gun to seek us out through the brush. Fatigue and thirst are forgotten.

Water trickling. We stop in place. The smell of the water causes an almost irresistible urge to run forward. Boxie, pointing at his eyes with his forked fingers, tiptoes away. A croaking bird. A squirrel rattles a branch as it jumps. A muffled voice not far off. Sweat bees hover almost motionless, close to my face, and I squeeze a red ant crawling on the back of my hand. One mistake, an accident, by one man—and it's all over. What are the odds against eight men not making a mistake?

Boxie returns. He points left and holds up three fingers, then right and two fingers. Knowing where and how many, we could eliminate them, but the noise would bring too much company. Boxie leading, we inch forward almost in a squat. Boxie half rises and points to his left front. Slowly, we follow. From a bush a few yards away comes the muffled sound of voices. I see the water for the first time. Not much, just two steps across. Boxie

---

* The paramilitary elements of the CIDG (Civilian Irregular Defense Group), a program begun by the Special Forces under CIA auspices to organize and train such ethnic groups as the Montagnards.

waits while Hoa carefully lays his weapon down, and takes out a hand grenade. The grenade poised, Boxie starts forward, giving his primary attention to the right flank.

One . . . two . . . he's across. A small eroded embankment. He reaches it and places his rifle on top. He feels around with his hands for a couple of seconds and then eases first one knee and then the other up over the top. Keeping his eyes to our right flank, he motions. I move forward, lay my rifle down, and take the grenade from Hoa, who traces Boxie's steps until they are together. The little Montagnard takes the grenade from me; it is my turn.

I'm at the embankment. I hand over my rifle and crawl up and through the others to take up position. After what seems hours we are all across and moving, again one step at a time. A twig snaps. We freeze, ears cocked. Will they take it for just a normal jungle noise? We start again. One meter, two meters, another. We can move a little easier now. An occasional twig snapping to their rear will be mistaken for one of their own members.

We must move quickly, get to the next stream before they discover we've slipped past this one. We have gained the top of the small ravine and are again on the flat. We move on for perhaps fifteen minutes and rest in place— hands relax a little on the weapons, legs are stretched out flat on the ground. Eight sagging, wilted bodies. I look at Grady: in addition to his obvious fatigue he looks filthy and cruddy; the beard doesn't help. I run my hand over my own face: I'll bet I'm no prize either. The Vietnamese, with barely a shadow of facial hair, look cleaner if no less pooped. The radio operator is propped back on his pack, head thrown back, eyes closed, mouth open, probably thinking of that water we passed over.

Three or four minutes and we're moving. It has been some time since we have heard a signal shot. Maybe it's our lucky day. I look at my watch: twelve-forty—Christ, we didn't make the 1000 contact. Couldn't have told them anything anyway, but they will be worried.

Moving slightly downhill, getting near the second stream. This one should be larger, which means it may be difficult to find a crossing with brush and trees to the edge of the water. The ground starts falling off on both sides and to our front. Another fairly steep cut to the stream bed. This time we are at a sharp bend on the triangular wedge which forces the stream to turn.

Boxie edges down the left slope, the point starts down the right. Again flies droning, birds screeching, more crawling ants, and leeches blindly but unerringly moving toward us, inchworm-fashion. Still no noise on our back-trail, no signal shots.

Brush moving. Weapons at the ready. Boxie, who has come up the opposite slope, starts toward Hoa. Then the point man appears silently. The two men crossed below: how did they keep from shooting each other when they met?

Boxie now moves the few feet to me. VC are at the bottom of the left slope; can't see any at the bottom of the right slope but can hear somebody further along. Perhaps we are lucky and there is a small break in their line. More water here, and more open. For perhaps eight paces we will be completely exposed. From where the point touches the stream at least two VC are visible. Again we must cross one at a time. The danger spot is not at the water but on the far side of the stream, where there is a dry sand and gravel bar that must be crossed. It looks hairy but Boxie is grinning, his gold teeth flashing. He reaches around behind him and produces his canteen.

He has water! I take two mouthfuls, one to slosh and one to swallow—it doesn't help much but seems to make breathing easier. He passes it to the others, grinning all the while.

We start down the right slope. I pause to listen to the rest of the team. I can't even hear Hoa in front of me or the radio operator behind me. The slight noise of leaves brushing over clothes and packs is absorbed by the jungle's normal din.

Boxie again has taken the lead from the point. The sound of their passing over rocks becomes clearly audible, and it will help cover some noise. We are on the bottom; trees are scarce but the ferns are thick and tall. We turn a little left now, following the base of the hill we descended. I glance up. The small ridgeline of the finger drops off suddenly. A few more steps and all that is left of the hill is an eroded bank. Motioning the others to stay in place, Boxie and Hoa move forward at a part stoop, part squat until they are at the lip of the bank. The stream cuts in close here. An inch at a time Boxie rises until he can look over the top of the bank. Back down, he turns and holds up four fingers. An internal hand grabs at my gut. My head turns in the other direction, listening.

Hoa looks over the bank and Boxie duck-walks almost to where it drops off. Can't swallow now, thumping heart has become the loudest sound in the jungle. Ahead of the little medic is the open space of the sand bar, but he doesn't start across. Still in a squat, never taking his eyes off the enemy position, he carefully takes out a canteen and lets the water run into the neck so it won't gurgle and bubble; switching his weapon to the other hand, he fills his second canteen.

Canteens secure, both hands on his weapon, he rises just a little and glances sidelong at Hoa, who has a grenade in his right hand, the pin already pulled. Hoa's weapon is propped against the bank beside him. Boxie stares toward the enemy nest for endless seconds, then turns to his right and starts walking, only partially crouched. He looks not at the enemy but ahead, to where he will be placing his feet. On the other side he disappears into the brush. Without seeing or hearing him, I know he will slowly make his way into a position where he can bring fire on the four VC.

I move forward now to replace Hoa. But with his head he motions me to pass. I don't argue and continue to the edge of the water. Slowly, I raise my head—my hat will keep my face in shadow. I almost involuntarily jerk my head back down: damn, they are close. Maybe ten meters, and I'm looking right at the back of one. Check my weapon. Reach around behind. Like Boxie, I start filling a canteen; unlike Boxie, I'm on my knees instead of in a squat. Now the other canteen. Eyes almost unblinking on the nest, I try to avoid looking directly at the man whose back is toward me.* The man changes position, there is a murmur of voices and a rustling of twigs and leaves. Freeze. They resettle. Now.

I rise almost to full height and reach into the water with one foot, groping for a flat rock. Can't muddy the water: it flows by our four friends. Now trail foot up alongside the first. Left foot high, take the next step. I'm in full view now. If our friend should turn around now . . . skin and muscle are knotted between my shoulders. Sand bar. Fight temptation: don't hurry, musn't scrunch. The ferns at last. Who would think I'd be glad to see brush and vines again?

* Scientific fact, superstition, or recurring coincidence: if you stare at someone long enough and with enough intensity, the subject becomes aware and will turn in your direction.

Next comes our Montagnard point. I motion him to go past, further into the brush and partway up the hill. Grady follows, and I move him off to a flank. There is a long break, but still no noise. Then suddenly the radio operator appears. Five across now. The rear men show up individually, and finally Hoa. Eight weapons to rattle, eight throats and noses to cough or sneeze, sixteen feet to stumble, but we made it. The crossing has taken thirty minutes.

Still with great caution we move up the hill. At the top we turn a little to our right and press on for perhaps five minutes. Staying in line, we stop and sit in position. Canteens out. Ahh . . . throats open again. Get a mouthful, move the head from side to side, let the lovely stuff get into all the dry corners. Swallow slowly. Tongues swipe at cracked lips. Salt tablets now. I take three, hoping my stomach can stand it. More water. I'm starting to sweat again. Grady has his eyes closed and is panting: cramps?

It would be nice just to sit here and doze and forget there is a war. So peaceful. Shake it off. Can't start thinking like that. Can't afford to lose the time we've gained. A last suck from the canteen and start moving again. It will be only a matter of time until somebody sees our footprints in the sand by the stream.

The ground is rougher here. The valley is narrowing. The hill mass to our right is steeper and seems to be pressing on us. Once in a while we can see the rise and a peak through a break in the trees. Can't get too close to the wall but must keep it in sight. Not likely they'll have another line here in the gap, but it's so narrow we could easily bump into casual traffic. The trail and the stream both have to share this narrow gap, leaving little room for error. Anyone guarding the gap will probably be high up on the cliff to our right. Must be careful to keep large trees overhead so anyone above won't see brush moving.

Keeping parallel to the cliffline, we seem to be turning more to the west. Yes. Now even more. The mountain line turns almost ninety degrees. We're through! We've done it! The valley, the ambushes, the rivers, the gap—all are behind us. There is a feeling of elation. After three days of being seconds from disaster it's hard to believe. Time for a short rest and then to find an LZ.

The interminable thorns grabbing and scratching. The back of my right hand looks like it has been worked on with a wood rasp. The vines continue to tangle our feet and snag pack buckles. It's lighter ahead, the trees are thinning. Two men deploy left and right. This trail is smaller than the earlier one, and we are hitting it diagonally: we are traveling a little west of southwest, the trail runs south of southwest. We start crossing. First one, then another, then a third. It's thin here so we move in further than usual and stop to wait for the others.

Footsteps. To our left front. Another path almost parallel to our course must run into the one we have just crossed. Not the fault of the man on the left flank, but if he had been further along he would have seen the junction. We are frozen in position but there is no way to warn the others behind us. The fourth man moves to join us; I put my hand up to stop him but it's too late. The steps stop. Inquiring voices, at least seven or eight. My eyes strain past the fern brush to the sound, searching. Orange. My eyes freeze on it: the brilliant orange of a jet pilot's suit in the jungle? Then a dark-blue movement to the side—a man stooping and weaving, searching. My feet are in a boxer's stance, weapon ready, my thumb having already moved the selector off "safe."

A face. The eyes lock onto my own. A look of absurd shock. Whatever he expected to see, it certainly wasn't a bearded "round-eye." For him it is the split-second hesitation that always proves fatal in a war, for in that fine second I fire: two at the dark blue; swing right, one at the orange. It disappears. By the time my third shot is on its way the whole jungle is in crescendo. The familiar sound of the three team weapons on my side. *Thunk* —one in the tree behind me. The acrid smell of the gunpowder. *Snick, snick*—brush being sliced with bullets. The peculiar *crack* of one close by which seems to create a vacuum in the ear. I'm still firing; how many rounds now? The laborious heavy banging of a submachine gun firing in bursts. The adrenalin is pumping, the eyes are clear, the mind works with fantastic speed and great clarity. An involuntary scream . . .

Hopefully the other four team members will go to the trail junction. If they do, they'll be able to get them on the flank. Keep moving around. An ejected casing hits the left side of my face. It's hard to pick targets through the brush, even harder to judge results. How long have we been shooting? Hope nobody's hit. Damn. From the corner of my eye I see the other four team members. Not their fault—they couldn't know about the path, but there goes our only chance to put a fast end to this. Keep firing even if no target. Fire is still coming at us but it is not aimed: most of it is high. The sound of a magazine being changed on my right. I think I still have two rounds left but change it now. A yell from the other side. The fire slackens.

I wave my arm. We start moving back, crouching, firing. Grady falls on my left. Hit? Son of a bitch! Now I'm down. My last shot went straight up in the air. A vine right behind the knees. I'm all tangled up. The tempo of firing increases from the other side. Leaves and brush are being cut down above me. It takes forever but I'm finally up and firing again. I note that two or three others are struggling to their feet, cursing in Vietnamese, Rhade,* French, and English—the same vine caught them. Keep backing away, keep firing. Our friends across the way are going to have lots of help soon. We have to get out of here.

We're only shooting at brush now. Turn and run. Avoid the thick brush. Must put distance between us. Christ! Another path. No time to scout—break through, and cross. Feet pounding. I turn back. I get to the path just as the two trail men send the staccato roar of automatic fire down the path: two VC running down the trail are hurled back, broken at the waist like rag dolls. Running again, we change direction, then slow down. Finally we stop, panting.

I look for Hoa. My heart stops: he's not here. Boxie is looking around too. Where is Hoa? He doesn't know. The point is also missing. What? I thought he was leading this parade. A phlegmatic shrug from Boxie—something he must have learned in the French Army.

We must go back; they may be wounded. I thought they left the firefight with us, but maybe I was wrong.

"No," says Boxie. "They not wounded. They go different way. We cannot find them. Maybe they ahead of us. We look, we in trouble."

"You're sure they're not wounded?"

"Sure."

* The Rhade, one of the three or four largest Montagnard tribes and considered to be the most sophisticated, are centered around Ban Me Thuot, 160 miles north of Saigon. Their language is of Malayo-Polynesian origin.

The other men confirm what Boxie has said. Grady? Another Gallic shrug. That's a big help. Is he learning from Boxie?

The decision is made. We move southwest again. On three sides we can hear occasional shouting and a random signal shot here and there. We move cautiously but quickly. It's getting late—only a couple of hours of light left. Without warning we almost walk into a large clearing. What a beautiful LZ. Maybe too beautiful and too large. We are at the north end, the mountain to our back. Keeping the clearing to our right, we start circling south.

It is taking precious time but we couldn't walk across the open area anyway. Noises from our rear are dying down. Taking count, reorganizing, getting ready for a sweep. They'll come slowly and with "safetys" off. The southern end of the clearing at last, and still no traffic.

"Boxie, set the big radio up. Get a helicopter in here fast. I'll get exact coordinates while you're setting up. Tell them if they can get a helicopter, any helicopter, in here within thirty minutes, we can get out. Grady, give them a hand with the antenna." I take out my map and compass and start taking an accurate fix on the peak to the north.

As I close the compass, Grady lays a hand on my shoulder. "We can't use the radio."

My head snaps around. "Why not?"

"This morning they distributed the operator's load. Some of the men took other stuff from him and Hoa took the long-wire antenna."

Grady looks desperate, his face pretty accurately reflecting my feelings. I don't even ask about the telescope antenna—never having had any luck with it in the past, we have long been out of the habit of carrying it. Well-intended solicitude for the radio operator has resulted in the breaking of a basic law: Never separate components. Take a deep breath. "Let's get the hell out of here. We're wasting time."

We probably couldn't have had a chopper here in time anyway. Philosophy? I make a mental note of this large LZ which has no prepared positions on its perimeter. It will be 2200 before we can make contact with the HT-1 radio. Another night and a very dangerous morning ahead of us, if we last that long.

We move west. The sun is getting lower, the jungle is in deep shadow. We will have to move until last light —no early camp tonight. Signal shots behind us, separate and from three well-spaced locations. In position and ready to sweep? I hope they are as far back as the sound indicates—maybe thirty minutes away—for they know our general direction. But this is their territory, and they know better than we do what lies ahead; they can afford to move leisurely.

Passing Boxie and taking the point, I push through some ferns and almost step onto a small path. I turn right; a little thicker here. Suddenly the ground drops off into what amounts to an overgrown ditch, running water at the bottom. We refill our canteens. Good maps we have —they show neither the large clearing nor this stream.

Up the other embankment. I stop, and Boxie almost runs into me. Smoke! I creep a few feet forward and slowly part the ferns. A small clearing and on the far side a "*hootch*" * tucked under the trees. We back off and turn left to circle. Tree cuttings are everywhere and the dried tops crisscross each other. The noise we make getting through seems horrendous so we turn a little further

* A G.I. term that can mean any type of abode but more correctly refers to a rude shelter of semi-permanent nature, and in this case a "house" made from at-hand jungle material.

left. Damn. Another path. We cross and move in a little further. We have to get away from the paths and streams. We don't know where they lead but our friends do, and the creek beds will be searched for sure.

Nuoc-mam. Then a little rattle. I freeze and motion with my hand. We all crouch and try to disappear into the ground. Footsteps now and the snapping of small twigs. One man. We hold our breath. I can see him but not clearly. I try to shrink deeper into the shadows. Black pajamas, a cartridge belt, and the sound of brush against metal. The odor is stronger. A glint of silver. He's carrying a food pot, four or five pans that fit together compactly with a carrying handle; no weapon. He is going to pass within feet of the last man. He's past, should be on the path now. I let my breath out slowly, look at my hand: it's holding my knife. I return it to its sheath and shudder; I don't remember taking it out.

The man who has just passed is taking dinner to a friend or has just picked it up at a communal pot. Either the word hasn't reached here or they don't expect us this far along—a small break for us. We move forward for another ten minutes and then come to another small clearing, and nearby a charcoal pit, loose wood stacked around it. We veer around. More dry treetops. Through that, then another small path. Turn again. Goddamn. We're back in the stream. Up the embankment. Peek through. I almost rear back on top of Boxie. I'm less than fifteen feet from an old man squatting, head bent over his bowl of rice. A twig snaps behind me. Chopsticks trailing some vegetable stop halfway to the old man's mouth. He finishes the motion and bends his head. Cool old bird. He knows someone or something is here but he's not going to let on. We slowly back away into the stream.

Down the stream, then out and up again. Another small clearing, another charcoal pit. They have been very careful cutting trees. They never clear a space large enough to let a helicopter sit down, and the overhang from the perimeter trees is enough to make the openings appear even smaller from the air. The area is a complete maze of paths connecting small clearings and *hootches*.

Another hour. Go forward, back off, circle, into the twisting stream, across more paths, veer left, cut right. Lateral movement more than equals our progress west. We still can't find a patch of uninterrupted jungle distant enough from clearings and paths to offer any amount of security for the night. None of the paths shows on the map and it is doubtful if they could be spotted from the air unless the observer knew exactly where to look.

In the last two hours we have traveled as far as we normally would in five, but damned little of it has brought us any closer to home. It is getting dark fast and we are at another path. Their pattern is now obvious: the smaller, less traveled paths are normally short and lead to *hootches* which are along the zigzagging streams; three or four smaller ones finally merge to form a larger trail leading to a charcoal clearing; still larger paths, some showing wagon-wheel marks and generally running west and east, seem to join the individual clearings.

We can hear voices on all sides. The smell of smoke from invisible cooking fires is everywhere. Frustration and fatigue increase. We are desperate. There is little more than pale skylight left now. In twenty minutes it will be pitch dark, and we will either have to stop then or travel on paths. Saigon has files jammed with ARVN survivors' reports testifying to the stupidity of that procedure.

We skirt a clearing and are at a small copse notable

for two things: cart-wheel tracks run parallel to it and there are innumerable felled treetops in it which almost form a barricade. Lousy cover, but we have no choice. I finally locate a small hole and duck in. Even darker here. I feel with my left hand; a snag scratches my face. It is really tangled. Slower. Feel ahead with my hand. A spot. I put one foot on it, bring the other alongside. Feel ahead again, move. I feel a nudge on my pack— Boxie staying close. I hope the others are doing the same.

We should be in about ten yards now. Better not go any further or we'll tumble out on the other side. Jesus, this stuff is noisy. I stop and slowly turn around. Boxie almost crawls over me. I pass him on. I stick out my hand and almost immediately a head is placed in it. Pass him on with a tap on the shoulder. Finally the fifth man. No broad circle tonight; all in one spot with bodies touching. Christ, we smell rotten.

I take off my pack with great care, take out my parka and radio, and refasten the pack. Slip into the parka and then back on with the pack. No luxuries tonight—no ground sheet. I won't be putting the radio back in the pack. I ease backward and almost lie on Grady. When I shift down, my right foot touches a shoulder. There is a head next to my left thigh and Boxie's head is resting on my right brisket. Sextuplets in a black womb.

Not too thick overhead. Branches move a little, probably from a slight breeze that we can't feel down here. I can see stars through the treetops. Grady is drinking water, very quietly. I try to relax but it's impossible. Voices drift to us from every direction. Occasionally we hear a shout. Voices approaching. Breath held. Closer . . . passing . . . gone. Boxie whispers "VC" in my ear. Who was he expecting?

Except for the sound of human voices it is quieter

here than in the deep jungle. I start drafting a message in my head and then rehearsing it. It has to be short but it must be understood. A funny sound from the man whose head is nested on my thigh. I put my hand out just as he rolls onto his side. A gushing noise followed instantly by a horrible stench: he's puking—just a few inches from me—and the stink of the fish and *nuoc-mam* in the vomit makes my own gorge rise. Another gushing. Gagging, I turn my head and strain for clear air, breathing through my mouth. Again. And the noise. It can't be helped but it seems that even if the people belonging to the night voices can't smell this putrid mess, they surely must be able to hear. Fear, nervous tension, fatigue. Finally his heaving subsides and he rolls back exhausted. I give him my canteen.

The drone of a plane. I bring the dial of my watch close to my face. Can't be ours—it's still an hour until contact time. It comes closer and a red clearance light blinks through the tops. The noise starts receding. Daylight! The whole fucking world is a white blaze. Every twig and branch is clearly etched. A goddamned flare. I'm staring straight up at it. I pull down a man starting to sit up. Why? Why of all places does a crew chief pick this place to kick out what must be a flare left over from some other mission? He couldn't have dropped it more squarely over us if he had used a sight.

With resignation to the inevitable comes dead calmness. The local folks will be here shortly. The flare is rocking on its parachute lines, moving shadows back and forth. I can hear voices shouting from every angle. Feet pound on hard paths. They will want the chute, and when it lands on us they will also want to put out the fire which will start when the flare hits these dry treetops. Any number of people are running back and forth ten yards in front of us at the edge of our hideaway—they are easily visible through the tangle.

A few seconds now and the flare will be on us, and that will surely be followed by a dozen unfriendly people crashing through. Wait—the shadows are longer. I glance up. The flare seems to be drifting northeast. The small night breeze has caught it. If only the chute doesn't burn before it clears us. Rocking away painfully slowly. Stops. It is snagged, maybe fifty yards away. Another few seconds and the light dies. There is a clamor of voices and all feet seem headed in that direction. I relax a little. My night vision is all screwed up: all I can see are fuzzy dancing red balls.

The voices subside—the people are moving off again. I keep rehearsing my message. I can see stars again. Look at my watch. With great care I get out of my pack and start rolling over on my stomach. The dried leaves are like corn flakes to roll on. I reach over and touch Boxie and Grady, who move their heads in. Propped on my elbows, I take a head in each hand and put my face between them: "When I talk on radio, cover my head with your bodies. Watch the antenna. Be quiet." Both heads nod.

I extend the antenna, fix the ear plug, and put my head down alongside my pack. I pull the parka hood over my head, turn on the set—and jerk as the rushing sound blasts my ear. Grady wraps his body around my head; Boxie lies partly on me and partly on Grady, taking the weight on his hands.

"Sunflower One, this is Gilded Cage. Over."

I don't answer. I am only going to say this once and I want to be heard five-by-five. The call signs are repeated. It has been a long time since they have heard from us and the tension in the operator's tone indicates that he really doesn't expect anything this time. Come a little closer, baby.

"Sunflower One, this is Gilded Cage. Over."

"This is Sunflower One. How copy? Over."

"This is Gilded Cage. Read you five-by. If you have traffic, am ready to copy. Over." He sounds excited. Probably pointing frantically to the radio to let others on the plane know he has made contact.

Slowly now, each word clear and distinct: "This is Sunflower One. Made enemy contact. Zero friendly killed. Zero wounded. Sunflower and Three missing. Am evading possible two companies Victor Charlie. They are all around. Many trails and houses under trees. Important. Important. Send chopper before . . ."

A hand squeezes my ribs.

". . . Wait." I turn down the volume.

Boxie whispers, "Light."

Footsteps go by on the trail.

Again in my ear, "Okay."

Up volume. "This is Sunflower. Over."

"This is Gilded Cage. Still read you five-by-five. Send your message. Over."

"Send chopper before first light. Must be in area of four one three niner before first light. Use Huey * with Hotel Tango One. Need guide and fix. Have Hotel Three Four near for fast pickup. Read back all after 'important.' Over."

"This is Gilded Cage. I read back: 'Send chopper before . . . fast pickup.' Break. If this is affirmative, signify by pushing button twice. Over."

Barely breathing, I push the button.

"Roger, Sunflower. Wait one. Break. This is Gilded

---

* UH-1B helicopter.

Cage. Over." A pause filled with the rushing of electrons in the atmosphere. "Roger. Break. Sunflower this is Gilded Cage. Push button if you read me. Over."

Again the button. Damn, it's close under here.

"This is Gilded Cage. Zimbalist * has monitored request and will comply. Over."

I push the button twice.

"Roger, Sunflower. See you in the morning. Good luck. Over."

I turn off the set and glance at my watch: less than five minutes for the whole transmission. I feel as if I've been under here for an hour. I butt with my head and the two men lift themselves. I collapse the antenna and start turning over on the leaves; stop. Wrong way—my nose tells me I almost rolled into the vomit. Finally I'm over and the pack is in place on my back.

Looking at the stars, I think of the TOC.† They will have to get a Huey tonight so they can strap on the external antenna for the HT-1 to the runner. Don't like using American pilots on these things,‡ but it has to be

---

* Code name of Operations Center.

† Tactical Operations Center.

‡ American pilots, having never worked with our teams, had no concept of what it was like to be on the ground. They had a propensity for arguing when our directions conflicted with the book. Working close in, they like to use gun ship escorts —fine for them but lousy for us. The VC know the pattern of U.S. choppers: a "slick ship" escorted by gun ships means a landing, so they immediately take position on likely LZs. U.S. pilots are loath to land on unsecured LZs without strafing, and they usually want more space than do our Vietnamese pilots. There are exceptions of course. The high quality of performance and outstanding selflessness of our Vietnamese pilots was considered exceptional. These remarks are not meant to impugn the bravery of U.S. pilots but to point out that our Vietnamese pilots were extraordinary with many years of combat experience.

a chopper and the Huey's turbine engine doesn't create static on the small radio. When they plot the coordinates I gave them, will they think it is our position? Even if I had light I couldn't fix our position closer than a hundred meters after all our meandering. The plot will bring them within hearing distance. I hope they realize they are going to be our eyes come daylight.

Grady stirs, and then, in a desperate whisper, "I have to take a crap."

I stiffen and reach up to pull his head down until his ear is next to my mouth. "Shit in your pants. You can't move."

He twists his head. "I can't hold it. Cramps are killing me. I'll be quiet."

Jesus Christ. Where do you find this in a manual—six men being compromised by unruly bowels. I hear him slip out of his pack and rise slowly to his feet. My body is rigid. Those small sounds fill the whole night. One cautious step and then another. My God, he's only three small steps from my head. The rustle of clothes. A poisonous effluvium bursts upon the area. I gag and twist my head to rid my nostrils of the putrid miasma. Only pinching my nose helps. He has more than a loose gut—it must be amoebic. Will he never finish? I apologize mentally to the nauseated Vietnamese at my side —by comparison his stink is nothing and Grady's emanations are like minor explosions—and I hope this won't start him puking again.

Grady is back in place. He had better drink plenty of water—we don't need a dehydrated man on our hands in the morning. I try to unwind, relax. What the hell, anything else tonight, even an attack, will be anticlimactic. I start cataloguing the night sounds.

No dozing tonight—can't chance someone rolling

over in his sleep or even breathing hard. Grady will probably sleep; he has had little sleep since we've been out. Should I take a couple of "Big Ds"? Better not. Want to stay awake but don't want to be jumpy or over-reactive.

Are Hoa and the point man all right? Actually, if neither is hurt, they are better off than we are. Two men make a hell of a lot less noise than six. They have a radio and if they monitor tomorrow, they can come out at the same place. They could have talked with the contact plane tonight. They may be closer to our pursuers and couldn't risk the noise.

What about the people searching for us? Are they still looking, using their perfume-bottle lamps to push back the darkness? Not very likely. Probably positioned in a huge semicircle. They will have all paths blocked and men along the stream lines. Are they down this far? They'll close the circle in the morning as more help arrives, but meanwhile they'll try to keep us moving away from the jungle and force us into the wide-open area four miles west. They'll be moving early. It's going to be close.

Cooler now. Those asleep will be restless. I listen to the breathing to anticipate movement. A small touch is enough to stop it. Grady is breathing deeply but not snoring; when it gets too deep, a touch is enough to raise his level of consciousness and reduce the noise. I am barely aware of the smells.

●   ●   ●

A small shake for each. Time to move. I am on my hands and knees. I make sure the waist strings on the parka are tight and slip the radio inside. Slowly. Patiently. Take it easy. Lots of time. Not even stars showing. One yard, another. Dead sticks jab at my face. I almost lose my hat to a thorn bush. Stop. A large thorn bush. A little right, slowly now. A little further right. Good. One more yard. Only the sound of brush lightly scraping against cloth disturbs the darkness.

A glance at my watch. We have been feeling our way for almost an hour. Another yard, more groping, more vines, more thorns. How much farther? Patience. Is it clearer ahead? I feel rather than see the opening beyond the treeline. I reach back and touch Boxie, indicating that he should stay in place. Yes, this is definitely lighter. Then I'm at a clearing. Inch around to the right. I can smell woodsmoke—it doesn't come from any particular place, but permeates the area. A distant voice calls out to someone. I have my hand on a path that seems to skirt the small clearing. The sky is less dark. I turn back. Ten minutes and I touch Boxie. We move almost to the treeline. I sit down and have the others bunch around me on their knees. Take out the radio—and wait.

"Sunflower, Sunflower, this is Bearclaw, Bearclaw. Over." They're here—some distance east and a little north of our position.

"This is Sunflower. I hear your station. Have pilot make tight orbit for one zero minutes. Directions to follow. Over."

"This is Bearclaw. Understand one zero minutes. Out."

Now, hopefully, the VC will think that a search plane is stupidly circling our position and will start moving to that area through the trees. Hopefully . . .

"Bearclaw, this is Sunflower. Over."

"This is Bearclaw. Over."

"I will give you a heading. When I say 'now,' mark your position and travel two more miles and swing north.

On 'execute,' take heading two six zero. Wait. Out."
The sound of the chopper motor increasing and ebbing
tells us it is orbiting. A couple of shots some distance
away. A signal? Ground features become more distinct
as the minutes creep by.

I set the compass at eighty degrees and wait until
the sound of the distant chopper is almost on line:
"Bearclaw, Bearclaw. Execute, execute. Over."

"Roger, Sunflower. Turning two six zero. Waiting.
Out."

It's getting close enough to hear the blades slapping
the air.

"You are getting close, Bearclaw. Readyyy . . . Now."

The Huey is over and gone. He isn't drawing any
small-arms fire in our vicinity. We can hear voices a
little east. I keep listening to the fading motor.

"Bearclaw turning north." I almost lose the sound
while he is turning. Wait. The morning twilight is well
on us.

"Bearclaw turning one four five." The increasing
sound of his engine confirms the message.

The chopper, after giving us our exact location, turns
to look for an LZ west of us but east of the large open
area showing on the map. I hang the radio by its strap
over my head and leave the earplug in place. Boxie leads
out to the east. We move quickly. The Huey has to be
our eyes and his flying time is limited.

Another path, another clearing, more dry brush and
treetops—a repeat of yesterday evening. The helicopter
comes close overhead and its passing produces excited
voices to our right. We now have the coordinates for
an LZ. Our airborne observer has also told us that there
is a cart trail on its north end, probably part of the
main trail in our area.

Boxie and Grady watch as I try to plot a course. Signal shots to the east—closer. Time to get moving again.

The radio blasts in my ear: "This is Bearclaw. Be careful. There is much smoke in your area. Over."

Smoke?—no shit.

"Check for movement ahead of us. Look close. Trails are hard to see. Out."

Vegetation is thin and continually cut by paths. The dry cut brush thrown back from the trails and small openings is becoming an increasing hazard: it is extremely noisy and at times blocks our way. Snags continually rip the plug from my ear. A completely irrelevant thought: Why haven't we heard the voices of any women in this jungle?

A patch of vines with the small thorns of wild raspberry has further irritated the back of my right hand. The canopy is getting thinner, letting through direct light; the temperature is rising. I'm sweating even more than usual because I'm still wearing the nylon parka. Hot air pushing up through the neck carries my own odor, which at this point is something else.

"This is Bearclaw. Four bandits on path moving east."

East? I motion and the team stops and gets down. I check my map. They must be close. Boxie looks at me inquiringly, and I show him four fingers and point. Footsteps in front—moving fast and getting close. The path is invisible, hidden by a wall of brown brush almost fifteen feet high stuffed in among the trees. They pass quickly, unseen, leaving in their place only the noise of birds, squirrels, and the distant helicopter.

We move on. The wall of brush on our right continues. The path must run parallel to our own course. The amount of light showing on our left indicates the possibility of a clearing or at least an area too open to traverse. We have been traveling almost two hours, stopping only to listen or let someone go by close to our position. The tension is evident in the animal reaction to an accidental snapping of a twig or the sudden chattering of a squirrel. I'm afraid fingers are getting too close to triggers—how many have their weapons on "safe"?

We are stopped by a high tangle of piled brush. We are on the inside of a corner. Boxie doesn't hesitate, gets out of his pack, and starts picking his way through the brittle branches. In a few minutes he is back and motions to me. I give my pack and radio to Grady and follow the little sergeant. It's like trying to tiptoe through a pile of crumpled cellophane resting on a bed of potato chips. Almost on our bellies, we reach the trail. It must be a main one. I stretch forward a little and look to the right —it joins the other trail which appears wider than the one in front of us. Across from us more dried brush and cut tops form brown corridors, as usual pushed back in far enough to be hidden from the air by the green treetops.

Boxie looks at me. It's an impasse. My turn to shrug, evoking a flash of gold from my companion. He knows as well as I do that walking parallel to a hidden path is as bad as walking on the path and we are wasting too much time getting through these barricades. We work our way back to the other four, and I retrieve my pack and radio.

Close to Grady I whisper, "Jack, you are about to do something this team hasn't done since the days we first started. We are going to walk on a blind trail in broad daylight. The brush is so thick that I don't think they'll have anybody in there. The danger will be from someone coming the other way or if we overtake someone. Don't worry about our rear unless we have to stop to check a crosstrail."

Boxie heads out, picking the quietest passage to the trail junction. He listens, takes a deep breath, steps out. I'm close behind. We almost run across the junction. Only the jiggling of equipment on our webbing tells of our flight. All across. I have the radio operator walk close on my heels to the left, since the static from the radio makes me deaf to the jungle on that side. Boxie is setting a fast pace, keeping well out from the sides. He has elected to keep away from fast cover in the brush in favor of the sandy track which muffles the sound of our boots. Does everyone feel as naked and vulnerable as I? Christ, that sun is hot.

The radio blasts on, telling me there is movement on the small backtrails. They are moving slowly, probably keeping pace with others searching the brush. We hurry forward.

Again the plug crackles in my ear: our flying eyes are getting low on fuel. We are close to a bend in the trail. They tell us that when the trail again turns west, in fifty meters, we will be at the LZ. I tell them to contact the H-34 and have them leave immediately: ". . . Have him make approach from south. Go home and thanks. Over."

"Roger. Good luck. We'll have the beer waiting. Out."

Hope we get to drink it. I yank the earplug out and stuff the radio inside my nylon steambath. I signal a tangent course with my hand, and Boxie finds a small hole in the crackly brush and moves through. Past the fallen tops it is fairly clear—ferns in abundance but not much else. We move on at a good pace. More dry fall ahead. Boxie guides to his right and in a few minutes waves at us to stop. He disappears. Then he's back, grinning, giving the "thumbs up." We're at the LZ.

We skirt the edge—can't bring the chopper in without checking. Finally we are at the western edge, where the trail returns to the jungle. We seem to have the area to ourselves. Expecting that any rescue attempt will be made by an armada, I suspect that the reception party will be three hundred meters further west, at the edge of the open area. We leave one man where he can observe the trail and still get out into the opening quickly.

We start backtracking and drop off the radio operator, who takes a position facing away from the open area. Grady and I stop halfway around and Boxie continues to the eastern side with the remaining man. When Boxie returns, we creep to the treeline and peer south. I get the radio out and affix the plug: nothing but static. Our eyes search the blue above the relatively low trees across from us. We gained time on the trail if they are beating the brush, but they can't be more than a mile behind.

The static stops—a Vietnamese voice. Hoa? I rip out the plug and shove the set at Boxie. As he listens, his face brightens and he is about to push the button. A frown. He looks up at me. "Not Hoa." He continues listening, the frown deepening. "Not Hoa. Ask for helicop. Maybe VC." He returns the radio.

Does this mean they've captured Hoa and have his radio? How long have they been on the air? I listen. A short message is being sent over and over with a short pause between repetitions. I leave the set on. Whoever it is, the signal is not too strong. Maybe it isn't Hoa's set. Could be a frequency close to our own with the sender nearby, and if he tries to sidetrack the chopper when it arrives, maybe I can override the signal.

Grady taps my shoulder and points. Two specks far south and quite high. I nod to Boxie, who is still frowning, thinking of Hoa. Grady and I slip into the open and across the trail into the grass—talk about sitting ducks. I sit down and Grady kneels close behind me, scanning the jungle. The specks have become miniature helicopters. The earplug is still repeating the message but there is no reply. If everything is SOP,* there will be one American and one Vietnamese in each chopper, both monitoring an HT-1. I dig the thick mirror with the peephole in the center from my shirt pocket. They are closer now but I still can't hear them. I check the angle of the sun and aim the mirror at the treetops opposite . . . have it . . . slowly I turn the mirror's white light to the choppers . . . that should be it . . . wiggle the mirror back and forth. The gap between the craft widens as the right one turns directly to us—he'll come in on a straight line, losing altitude as he comes; the other will make a fake approach on a larger field.

It must be the *Dai-uy*—the Captain,† or else he wouldn't have turned so fast—it's his mirror. I give him another flash, since he won't be able to see this clearing until he is almost on it. Suddenly there is a loud Vietnamese voice in my ear—someone answering our unknown broadcaster. The weaker signal comes in, a longer message this time.

At the break I key in: "This is Sunflower. Tell Vietnamese to ignore last message. Enemy on same frequency. May have SOI.‡" The other chopper changes direction. "Do you roger? Over."

"Roger, Sunflower. Counterpart in other bird. Will relay through pilot. Out."

* Standard Operating Procedure.
† At the time most of our pilots were still lieutenants; some had held that rank since Nguyen Cao Ky had been one.
‡ Signal Operating Instructions—paper showing frequencies, call signs, and authentication and coordinate codes.

Off to the west the second chopper suddenly lifts up and peels to his left. My eyes come back to our bird: he's much closer and the noise of the motor is quite audible. I unroll the colored panel.

"This is Streetcar. We see your panel. Coming in. Out."

I stuff the panel in my jacket, turn my back, and get up on one knee facing the trees where the trail joins the clearing. Grady is covering the right. The motor becomes a roar; the rpm changes violently and the four blades pound the air savagely. A blast of air hits my back. The man posted on the trail leaps into the open and charges forward. From the corner of my eye I can see the radio operator doing the same thing.

The airframe of the bird vibrates behind me. How far into the red is the manifold needle? The prop blast has the grass completely flattened. What a target. The two men, not glancing back, almost converge on me and charge past. Slap Grady, up—spin and run. Grady is a few steps ahead of me, weapon on "safe." I unsling the radio with my left hand, drive. Ahead, Boxie's face peers out from the shadow of the door. At four feet I start my weapon and radio on their way. At two feet I dive head-first into the tangle of bodies . . . hands grab for me . . . the chopper is up and turning. Ragged rifle fire follows—and then there is only the noise of the motor. We made it.

I roll over. Boxie has his arms around me, kissing me on the head and cheeks. Other hands are pounding me, and the plump crew chief is grinning from under his visored space helmet. It's still not real—even the cool air from the door fails to make our safety real.

Suddenly the crew chief is shaking my arm. He

gives me the helmet. The pilot wants me on the intercom.

"Hi, Dai-uy. What's up?"

"Other plane pick up lieutenant and other man. Take many bullet holes but everybody okay."

I don't answer. I rip off the helmet and shout the news to Boxie. Everybody is babbling and pounding each other. Boxie is holding my hand with both of his.

The crew chief shakes me again and points to the left-hand windows. I twist around just in time to see a fleet of armed Huey's—gun ships—with their rocket pods uncovered. I sober. The war isn't over. They are speeding to our vacated area to unload at unseen targets.

●　　●　　●

There is an old man squatting, head bent over his bowl of rice . . .

HOW DID YOU HAPPEN to have the mirror?" Manny asked.

We were in the cool dim club. I was on my second gin and tonic, Manny was drinking Scotch. It was two hours since the chopper landed. A happy reunion with Hoa, a short debriefing, shower, shave, clean clothes: unwinding time. I had been giving Manny a recap of the mission while downing steak and eggs. Grady and Kovacs, Manny's assistant, were behind us at the bar, swapping tales with much arm waving.

"Vinh gave it to me just before we left."

"Cowboy?" (A nickname given to the Captain when he first came to this project, wearing a bush hat and low-slung revolver.) "How did that happen?"

"It's his survival mirror. Just before we loaded he handed it to me, saying he can see it further and doesn't have to depend on radio directions from the cabin. Says he knows how to get in better than any radio operator. 'Course he's right. It sure beats using a smoke grenade."

"Anything beats using a smoke grenade," Manny agreed. "You know, of course, that he thinks we're both crazy."

"I know. He says we go too often. He should talk. He was almost right this time, though. We were damned lucky. You weren't quite so blessed, Manny—one killed, one wounded. It sounded like a hell of a fight. What happened?"

"Well, our main objective was that lone knobby hill the other side of your western ridge. As we surmised from the briefing, it was loaded. When we landed, we may have been observed from above. The next day we reached the slopes and it was almost impossible to get up. You've never seen vines and brush so thick. We had to keep circling because it was so steep, even though it meant crossing paths."

"Must have been fun sleeping that night."

"It was. Damned near had to tie ourselves to trees to stay on the hill. We could hear voices every so often and other noises from uphill."

"From the temple they said was up there?"

"Probably. I think they use it for a lookout." Manny looked grim. "We had signal shots too. Every time a plane came within sight or hearing, somebody would fire a round. The next day it was more struggling. In the afternoon we stumbled on a spring with a number of paths leading to it—we couldn't watch them all but we needed water, badly. We had almost filled our canteens when a monk walked up. One look and he hotfooted it. There was no chance to grab him, and shooting him wouldn't have helped us, since there was the chance that he was neutral and wouldn't report."

"Sounds familiar, Manny. Like when we were spotted in that valley west of Dang Ba Thin. What can you do? It's still the best choice."

"We got out of there fast," he continued, "but kept moving. About forty minutes later we were stopped by brush and vines so thick it was impossible to push through."

The half dozen men from the other field teams were pulling up chairs. The waitress pushed through and set new drinks on the table for us.

"We had a choice—either take the trail or go through a rock cut, so we took the rocks." He paused to take a drink. Some commo * and other non-field types pressed a little closer. "Without warning, all hell cut loose. They were firing from above. We started shooting but couldn't really see them. Bullets were bouncing everywhere. The team leader, who had been doing a great job, turned the team and moved them back. We hadn't gone ten steps when the point man was zapped and thrown back. The team leader turned and looked at me, his eyes as big as coconuts, and threw up his hands. I had to take over. First, I helped put the wounded man on Kovacs' back and . . ."

Kovacs' heavy Central European accent broke in: "I could not believe my eyes. Manny turned around and started running through the cut, firing like mad. Bullets were spraying in all directions. We all started running behind him, everybody shooting."

Manny continued: "I guess they didn't expect us to try and force through that way. We got to the end of the cut and turned downhill. One other man got hit but it was in the arm."

"Damn miracle," I said. "Why the hell didn't they lob a few grenades at you?"

Manny shrugged.

Kovacs spoke up. "Pretty soon we had to stop. The guy on my back weighed a ton. He had been hit in the gut and the leg. He was trying to talk."

"I asked the team leader what he said," Manny in-

* Communications-radio operators.

terrupted. "He said, 'He not live, must leave him here and run.' I had thought of that. We could still hear random shots and people shouting and crackling brush behind us, and carrying a man through the brush was going to be slow if not impossible; but when I heard what the guy had to say, there was no choice. We stripped off all his gear and gave him two syrettes of morphine. I picked him up, gave Kovacs my pack, and we kept going. When it started to get dark, we couldn't stop—so, like you, we did the unforgivable and started using trails. I still can't figure why they weren't blocked. Anyway, it took no time to get to the bottom, and we just kept moving. At the twenty-two-hundred contact we told them what had happened and to have helicopters ready in case we could get to an LZ."

"You should have seen the flap that traffic caused here," a commo man contributed. "They even alerted two Ranger companies to stand by. Only problem was, they didn't have enough aircraft to move them anywhere."

Manny smiled and continued, "We kept pushing on. After it got dark, those chasing us moved a little slower but they were never far behind. We finally made it to the highway around midnight."

"Midnight!" I exclaimed. "Christ almighty, you must have been running. You carry that guy all the way?"

He nodded. "As soon as we arrived we set up the 162 * and started calling for a chopper. The man I was carrying was unconscious, in pretty bad shape—there isn't much you can do for a gut wound, and being bounced on my shoulder didn't help—and I was completely covered with his blood. While we were still on

---

* HC-162D—single side-band radio, which has self-contained batteries and can send voice or CW. Simple to operate, its range is virtually unlimited.

the radio a truck came along and the Vietnamese wanted to flag it, but I put thumbs down on that idea. It went around the next turn and about a minute later—*bam*. 'Charlie' had an ambush set up, and that was the end of the truck. The rest was pretty routine. The chopper arrived and landed right beside the road. The man died about fifteen minutes before it got there. Taking off, we took four hits from rifle fire but no real damage. The man hit in the arm didn't have any broken bones and he's walking around with a sling." Manny took a long pull from his drink.

"Sounds like you're damned lucky it wasn't worse, but one dead and one wounded . . . How's the Vietnamese morale?"

"They're shook up," Kovacs answered, "but they think Manny is some sort of god. The project still has a perfect score: we've never left a body, dead or wounded, behind. They thought they were all going to be dead men back in the rocks. We would have been, too, if not for Manny. I thought he was committing suicide when he ran right at them. It's getting embarrassing for him. Every time one of the Vietnamese sees him he grabs his hand, holds onto his arm, pats him on the back. As far as they're concerned he couldn't do anything wrong if he tried. They lost a man but they are sure a happy group."

"Why not? Next to wanting to live, the most important thing to them is what happens to their bodies after they're dead. The VC even have special people detailed for body recovery in a battle. Except for the Irish, I don't know anybody who enjoys a good funeral more."

Kovacs, back at the bar with Jack Grailey and Terry Adams, was repeating the episode with embellishments and virtuoso arm waving. In contrast to his listeners, who had weight-lifter builds, he looked overweight, paunchy. I could tell by the way Grailey perched forward on his stool that it wouldn't be long before he interrupted with his last mission's exploits. Manny looked over at them and smiled. His glance shifted to where Grady was reliving our firefight for Bill Kane.

"Hey, Wurley, if we sit here long enough we're going to hear a war story. Let's go downtown," Dixon suggested.

"Okay. See you guys later," said Wurley with a wave.

Manny stopped them on their boisterous way out. "Don't get your heads bad—you may be going in tomorrow. And stay away from the MPs in those camouflage fatigues. If you see Trulow in town, give him the same message."

Blythe spoke across to Curtis: "Why don't we go too, Allen? Let's give the local economy a boost with a low-level leaflet drop.* Can't let the couth-and-culture kids get head of us." He jerked his thumb toward the departing Dixon and Wurley.

Curtis looked at his watch. "Small drop? Starting this early we could set a new track record. Hell, why not? How about you, Manny? Dunc? Anybody else want to go downtown?"

"No thanks. It's quieter, cooler, and cheaper right here. We can't compete in the same bar the way you guys throw your personality around."

In a few seconds we could hear a jeep cranking up and driving off. Bill Kane joined us. I turned to Manny: "I swear I don't know how those two do it. Since I've

---

* A leaflet drop would normally refer to propaganda leaflets being dropped from an airplane. Here it refers to the custom in most Vietnamese bars for keeping tabs on drinks: with each drink you receive a leaflet about three inches square marked with the price is tucked under an ashtray; tally is made when you leave. Each drink (Saigon tea) bought for a "hostess" is on a separate leaflet marked with her initials.

known them I haven't seen either one spend less than fifteen dollars a day picking up leaflets."

Manny snorted. "Well, on per diem you could do it, too. Figure how much they spend beyond that—they probably average less than we. They do the same thing in Okinawa, so they have to come back here every six months just to stay even."

"Manny, do you ever wonder why those just back from a mission seldom go to town the same night?"

Manny's black eyes stared at me for a second before he answered. "What's there to think about? They're tired."

"Sure, but I think it's more than that. For some reason . . . we have to talk and we drink more. Even you talk more than normal."

Manny flushed a little under his tan and his voice was edgy: "Did you ever think that after whispering for four or five days, it's just a pleasure to talk out loud —like clearing your throat."

"Maybe," said Kane, "but I doubt it. Those who do go to town don't go to find women, even the cockhounds. You can almost tell how bad a mission was by how long and how loud we talk after we get back. Listen to those two at the bar: offhand I'd say Kovacs was pretty damned scared out there—he's still talking and he's been back over twenty-four hours."

Manny glanced at Kovacs and Grady and leaned forward. "Of course he was scared—we all were. This isn't like Korea, Kane. This is the first war I know of where a ground soldier can be in the middle of the blood, stink, and death one minute and be in a cool bar drinking a gin and tonic twenty minutes later. It takes time to unwind."

"A good point," Kane agreed, grinning. He had

eighteen years of service—over half his life in the army —but he was the youngest of the three.

"If you mean that in Korea soldiers had more time to unwind before they had a chance at the fleshpots, it's a good point," I said.

"I don't follow that," said Manny, signaling for another round.

"Think of it this way, Manny. You were scared in Korea and you're scared here. In Korea it took many hours, sometimes days, after prolonged fear before you could get to women. Here it's immediate, but we have to talk it out before we want to head for the girls. We don't want the women until we've rid ourselves of the fear or the tensions caused by the fear."

"That doesn't make sense," said Manny, and the men who had edged back to the area of our table nodded in agreement. "They don't sit around saying how brave they are—just the opposite. I admit I'm scared when I talk about a mission and so do you; so do Kovacs and Grady."

"That's just it, Manny," Bill broke in. "We all know we're scared so there is no real reason to mention it, but we do, because if we say it often enough, it loses reality and we quit believing it. Of course, there is always the possibility that as long as we have a mission, we don't need sex."

Some of the bystanders laughed, and even Manny managed a small grin. "Thank you, Mr. Freud," he cracked. "And how do you figure that?"

"Actually, it's the same thing—not just another possibility. Cowboy is right: we are nuts. A psychologist could have a field day with us." I paused to drink. "Every time we go in we know we are going to be scared, and we are. We're all volunteers on this project—we don't have to go in, but we do. Why?"

"Well, there's always duty, honor, country," Bill suggested, grinning.

Manny broke into the listeners' laughter: "Save that for the TI and E classes.* We go because it's our job and we're good at it—we're professionals. It's our skill against the VC. We're proving that a small group can move around in the VC's home area and effectively beat him at his own game."

"That's what and how, not why," I corrected. "What we are and how we operate. Sure we have the skills—and thousands of dollars' worth of sophisticated radios, helicopters, C-47s to fly contacts, choppers to stand by in case we get in trouble, helicopters to bring us home. With all that going for us, if we survive the first couple of hours, we have a fifty-fifty chance of getting out five days later. We have to be skillful with our equipment, because it's all we've got. As we've learned the hard way, nobody living in the area will help us. The VC have the people, we have our helicopters. I don't call that effective, and I don't think it's the same game."

"I still say as individuals we're better in the jungle than the VC—we move faster and shoot better," Manny declared emphatically.

"Oh, I agree. Considering how many they are and how few we go in with, and figuring they know all the paths and trails and we still evade after they know we are in the area proves it. Also . . ."

"That's all very interesting," said Bill, "but it's getting away from the subject. Why do you think we keep going on these missions, Dunc?"

"It's very close to what you said about sex, Bill. Fear makes us go back."

* Troop Information and Education.

Manny snorted. "That sounds like doubletalk: because we're afraid, we go on a mission so we can be afraid."

"I think Dunc's talking about two different kinds of fear," Kane offered.

"Fear is fear," said Manny. "The only difference is in degree. Some people are more afraid than others and sometimes the same person is more scared than at other times."

"I think you're wrong, Manny," I said. "There are many kinds even if they are related, but let's just talk about two. What is it that we fear on a mission?"

"Dying—getting killed, I suppose," Manny answered.

"Right. Death. And as the book says, it's that fear that helps us survive. Still, we hate it; we resent it because it makes us feel less like men."

For an instant my mind flashed back to the stream when I had had to step out into the open. I wondered why when you're scared in a situation like that, you always feel naked, with that crawly feeling in your scrotum and an almost irresistible urge to hold onto, to protect, your privates.

"The fear that makes us go back again and again is stronger than our fear of dying or death: it's the fear of losing our manhood."

"Come off it, Dunc," Manny said, "I don't have to prove I'm a man and neither do you—none of us does."

"Right, but we do. We don't have to convince anybody else, so we must be trying to convince ourselves."

"Think of it this way, Manny," Kane said. "In jump school any number of people were scared shitless, but they jumped—because they were told over and over that everybody was just as scared, but a 'man' jumps anyway. The idea being that if they followed their instincts and didn't jump, they just weren't men. So they jumped—because the thought of quitting and losing their manhood was worse than the thought of being splattered over a drop zone."

"Well, I suppose that's true," Manny admitted grudgingly, "but do you really think that's the same thing?"

"Sure," Bill answered. "It's no more natural for a man to step out of an airplane at a thousand feet than it is for him to stand up and make himself a target. You do both to prove something."

"That's right," I said. "Knowing we're not going to like it, we volunteer to go again. The alternative is to quit, but we prefer to go because although no one would blame us if we did quit, we would doubt our own manhood. So by talking long enough, we assure ourselves we are men—and we don't want women until we do."

Manny was getting annoyed. "I still say it's only because they're tired."

"I never notice anyone in a big hurry to get to bed, but you can always bet your sweet ass that most will be in town the next day looking for some womb to climb into."

Everyone laughed at Kane's remarks, and the tension was broken. He could say the damnedest things and a person was never sure if he really knew what he was saying. Those standing around began drifting off to other tables.

Manny picked up the conversation. "I'll bet there is some great ass-chewing going on in your area right now, Dunc."

"You mean about the two ambushes?"

"Right. Whoever was in charge there must really be getting reamed out. Must have been quite a shock to find you had slipped through."

"I guess so." I smiled. "The way those guys we had the firefight with were walking along and talking, I guess we weren't supposed to be anywhere in the area."

"It must have looked like a Chinese fire drill * back on the river when the shooting started," said Bill. "They probably couldn't believe you had sneaked past, and thought someone else was doing the shooting—probably what saved your ass. I can see them now, milling around and arguing and then trying to get organized after they got the word from the main man."

"How was Grady?" asked Manny. "Will he make a first man?"

"He was good. Hear what he's talking about now—crossing those streams and diddlybopping past the VC? There's a lot of training behind that maneuver. It's a little hard to tell about him being a first. He reacted well —shot when he should and didn't when he shouldn't. But he's going to have to learn to sleep out there. Right now I think he's afraid to sleep for fear something might happen and he won't know it, like the rest of us when we got started. If he lasts, he'll know if he can handle a team. Meantime he'll make a good number two. How about Kovacs?"

Manny grinned. "I think he's going to be real good. He's a little out of shape and sweated blood, but kept up. Sure glad he wasn't one of those hit. Can you imagine having to carry a load like that? If you or I get hit, the Vietnamese could carry us, but Kovacs is in a strain if he ever gets it. He's not ready for his own team, yet, but I think he will be in one or two trips."

"Now that we're out and know 'Charlie' is in there, Manny, are the troops going in to get them?" I asked.

* Term used to express hopeless milling and confusion.

"Doesn't look like it," he said disgustedly. "It's the same old crap—troops aren't ready, not enough helicopters, need them someplace else. You name it, they have no shortage of reasons for not going in. It's like you said in the intelligence briefing before we left: 'If you're so goddamned sure they're in there, why send eight men? Send a battalion!' They won't even bomb the mountain we were on because of the temple—the temple belonging to the monk who put the bad mouth on us."

"It's starting to give me a bad case of the royal ass," I blurted. "What the hell is the sense of somebody going in to confirm confirmed intelligence if they don't plan on reacting? Sixteen people risked for nothing—again. They always tell us what they're going to do if we find something and then—nothing. The thing that grabs me is rushing us in before we could really study the area."

"In briefing you said there was something about your area that stank," Manny recalled. "I thought maybe it was because it wasn't your team's turn to go in and you only had three days' rest. Was the gap really that narrow?"

"Narrow. I hope to kiss your sweet ass if it wasn't. You can't see it from the air because of the way the trees grow—they are tall on the floor of the valley, and they get progressively smaller the further up the hill they go from water—which is what made it look so wide. All we managed to do is stir our friends up. They'll either move or dig in so hard hell won't move them." I drained my glass and ordered another round.

Dave Lawson, a clerk from TOC, walked in and stopped, squinting into the gloom. He spotted our table and came over, grinning. "Manny, the Vietnamese are having a ceremony tomorrow morning. They are going to give you and Hunky a medal."

Hearing his nickname, Kovacs came over and asked, "What kind of medal?"

"I'm not too sure, but I think it's a bronze star for you and a silver star for Manny."

Manny broke in before Kovacs could reply. "Kovacs, do you have any plans to go someplace for the next few days?"

He shook his head, and Manny turned to me, "How about you Dunc, any big plans?"

"Other than picking up some beach time, none. Why?"

"I have to go to Saigon for a few days and one of us should be here to keep an eye on things in case they do send in the other teams."

Dave spoke up, "You don't have to go to Saigon. The ceremony is going to be right here."

"I know. That's why I have to go to Saigon." Manny looked at Kovacs and added, "Hunky, as long as you don't have any other plans you can accept for both of us."

Kovacs' excitement changed to confusion, and he looked as if he had been trapped and wasn't sure how or why. To Lawson, a man who kept a minute account of his flying time in order to be eligible for an Air Medal, Manny's attitude was beyond comprehension. The two men left the table and retreated to the bar.

"How are you going to get to Saigon, Manny?" Kane asked.

"One of the choppers is leaving soon to pick up the dead man's widow and bring her here. That's another scene I'd just as soon miss." Manny glanced at his watch and pushed back his chair. "I'd better get a bag packed and tell the pilot I'm going. Dunc, how about you and Bill making sure Kovacs doesn't get so drunk he forgets the team party tonight? I'll see you in a couple of days."

"Okay, Manny. Have a ball. If anything drastic happens, I'll leave word with the TOC on Pasteur Street."

Kane and I went back to discussing the highlights of the last few days. The story of the sick Vietnamese and Grady's loose bowels had gained color with repetition, and now that the tension and stink were fading from memory, I could laugh with Kane as I told it.

"Have you said anything to Grady about it since you've been back?" Bill asked.

"Hell, what's the point? He must be pretty embarrassed about it. You'll notice he doesn't say much about it to the others. It's not as if he had some devious plot to hold back, just waiting for a chance to shit on me."

Laughing, Bill leaned forward and asked, "Think it was fear?"

"I suppose. Lack of sleep, tension, too much water on an empty stomach, or a combination. Who knows? Why should he have been the only one not afraid that night? Our chances of making it through the night were pretty remote and the chances of getting out this morning were nil. When I'm scared, I have just the opposite problem."

"I know what you mean, Dunc. I'm the same way. I get in a position like that and you couldn't drive a needle up my ass with a twelve-pound sledge."

We laughed and ordered another round.

"Bill, let's go stand at the bar. If I keep drinking like this, I'll never get out of this chair."

He nodded, and we picked up glasses and cigarettes and joined the others. Grailey was in the middle of his last mission and Kovacs was only half listening, impatiently waiting to have his turn again.

"I guess I'd better slack off on this," I said, swirling the ice. "My team is having a party tonight, too. The Vietnamese are running around now, setting it up in a small restaurant."

"How much money are they going to get for this trip?"

"Mmmm—hard to say. We can be sure of three kills in the firefight, and counting the two we zapped on the path later, that would be five thousand piastres.* I imagine they'll convince the wheels that they got at least ten, so that would double it. Same for Manny's team."

"Should be a pretty good-sized party," Bill observed. "They'll probably get more than that to offset any gloom for losing the one man. Both teams going to be at the same place?"

"I doubt it. Everybody will get a hero's toast and there will be the usual flowery speeches to the bunch for being the best team. Can't do that with two of them present. I'll probably have to drop by and have a drink with Manny and Kovacs' team."

"Why? Because Manny won't be there?"

"Partly," I answered, "but mostly because before Manny came, I went out with them. They'll expect me to show."

"I didn't know you were with that team. I thought you had always been with the one you have now."

"It was back when Project Delta was having it's birth pains. We were rebuilding after the Laos fiasco. We didn't have staff and field sections then, so we did both jobs. There were only fourteen of us and only one American went with each team. When the wheels in Saigon heard about it, they said it was too dangerous for an American to go alone with the Vietnamese, so we had to double up, which meant going on twice as many trips. We used to

---

* The official exchange rate was 72 piastres to the dollar; the black market rate was 125–140 to the dollar; and the rate to the U.S. military was 56 if purchased from Vietnamese authorities.

go with one team and then on the next trip with another. Manny's team was my alternate."

"Nice vote of confidence for the Vietnamese. I thought the 'two Americans' rule was in force long before that."

"It was but we ignored it. Actually it was a good morale thing, because it showed the Vietnamese we trusted them. I think the wheels knew it and just didn't say anything."

"What made them change their minds?"

"There was a feeling, not without good reason, that the Vietnamese were unhappy because we screwed them on the Laos infiltration. We were supposed to go with them and didn't, and as you know most of them never came back. After that the powers-that-be thought it was too dangerous. When we tried to argue, they told us they would have stopped it sooner had they known about it."

"Damn," Kane exclaimed. "Twice as many trips—and you've been doing this since it started. How many missions have you had?"

"Who counts? Besides, it didn't seem as dangerous then. You may not realize it, but for the past few months we have been going into increasingly hostile areas— ARVN troops haven't dared for years to go where we go now. Back then, we were strictly reconnaissance teams. This 'hunter-killer' concept didn't come until later. Now we have more men for field teams and we have commo and operations separate from the teams, so we don't have to do both ends of the operation."

"What is it the NLF radio called us—'Suicide Squads'?"

I smiled. "Right, and considering what we have planned for the future, 'Charlie' may be right."

We lapsed into silence.

I was in the midst of analyzing my reactions in the

firefight when Kane broke into my thoughts: "Dunc, do you think it's worth it?"

Kovacs stopped what he was saying, jerked around, and asked the question for me: "What do you mean, 'Do you think it's worth it?'"

Bill stared at his drink for a minute and then lifted his head. "I mean a lot of things. Is it worth risking our necks to get information and then have nobody do anything about it, for instance? Is it worth being here at all? This is my third trip to Viet-Nam, and your second, Hunky. Are things any better now than when you first came here?"

"It's not for me to say. It's not for you to say either."

"Why not, Kovacs?" I asked. "It's a good question. Are things any better than, let's say, a year ago? Why don't the Vietnamese act on our information?"

"We don't know everything. Maybe they have very good reasons for not doing anything," Kovacs said belligerently.

"That's bat shit and you know it, Hunky," Bill said. "They have never given us a good reason for not following up on our missions. The couple of times they have gone out it took them three days to get started and they advertised it so well they never found anything."

"Maybe they have information we don't about the area and that's why they don't go." Kovacs looked unhappy.

"Wrong again, Hunky. The problem is they know exactly what we know after we come out: they know for sure the VC are there and will fight, they know that they outnumber the VC, and they know they don't want to fight the VC." Bill, his drink forgotten, jabbed the air with his middle finger to emphasize his charges. "And, there is one other point you should know, if after all this time you don't: the only reason these people fight at all is because we're here."

"That's not true," shouted Kovacs, crashing his hand on the bar. "They will fight."

"Sure," Bill replied, almost soothingly. "When they have no choice or they're wrecking some town or terrorizing women on the street. How well did they fight at Hiep Hoa? * The only reason you didn't get captured along with the other four Americans was because you were out on patrol. Why wouldn't the Vietnamese commander bring the patrol back to help the camp? Why didn't the ARVN force down the road help the camp?"

The argument halted other conversations, and men started drifting over. Bill Kane had really hit a tender spot when he brought Hiep Hoa into the discussion. Kovacs was getting red in the face.

Kane prodded: "The only reason the VC attacked at all was that they knew ARVN wouldn't move before morning, if at all."

"They couldn't leave their place undefended," Kovacs burst out.

"A sugar mill? Big deal." Kane pressed on. "Hunky, do you have any idea why we are here?"

"Of course I know. MACV † sent us here to do a job."

"I don't mean in this specific place. I mean why any of us are in Viet-Nam."

---

* Hiep Hoa, on the Vam Co Dang River northwest of Saigon, was the site of a Special Forces camp overrun in November 1963. Four Americans and a substantial number of weapons were captured. Of the four, Sergeant Rorback was reported shot in September 1965 in reprisal for the execution of a VC agent; Sergeant Camancho escaped in August 1965; Sergeants Smith and McClure were released by the Viet Cong in November 1965.
† U.S. Military Assistance Command, Viet-Nam.

Sharp grunts from the bystanders. The conversation was taking an unpleasant turn. Baiting Kovacs was one thing, but this was getting out of hand. Sympathy was swinging to Kovacs and only Kane's combat record kept him from being shouted down.

Kovacs almost exploded. "Of course I know why we're here—to fight the Viet Cong—" He crashed his hand on the bar and made the glasses jump.

"Who are the Viet Cong, Hunky?" The louder Kovacs shouted, the quieter Kane became.

"The commies . . . the enemy . . . the people trying to overthrow the government . . ."

"Did you ever stop and think," Kane interrupted, "that the reason they fight the government is that they know it's as rotten as we do?"

Kovacs looked ready to take a swing at Kane. "What makes you think you're so goddamned smart? If there wasn't good reason for being here, we wouldn't . . . You think you're smarter than the President?"

The crowd was on Kovacs' side. He smiled in smug triumph. I had never heard Kane speak out like this; he had an almost beatific smile on his face. I thought he would ignore the question but he threw it right back.

"Ah, that's why you are here, Hunky. The President sent you. Being God, he's infallible."

Not expecting an answer, Kovacs looked confused for a moment and the blood rose again in his face. "You and your fancy fuckin' words. You and Duncan may read a lot of books but you only think you're smart. The President knows a lot more about Viet-Nam than both of you put together."

It was my turn. "Hunky, he knows about Viet-Nam exactly what people want him to know. It's people like us who gather the information, and you know that no matter how bad the reports are, somebody can always reword them to sound cheery."

Kovacs glared at me and shouted, "You both talk like traitors . . . like"—he groped for the worst thing he could say and finished with a burst—"like *beatniks!*"

Kane, probably thinking of his eighteen years in uniform, almost choked. He recovered enough to ask, "Why are we traitors, Hunky?"

"Because you're talking about such things. The President is the Commander-in-Chief—if he says 'Go to Viet-Nam,' we go to Viet-Nam. You should not ask why. You are a soldier. You obey orders . . . you fight . . . you are not paid to think . . ."

Again Bill interrupted, "Come off it, Hunky." He was really leaning on Kovacs' nickname. "You aren't talking to a basic trainee. If . . ."

Kovacs broke in, "The President was elected by the people to be our Commander-in-Chief. If you question the President, you are against democracy. Besides, if we don't fight them . . ."

"Yeah, I know, Hunky, 'we'll have to fight them in California.' Now why don't you say something you thought of?" I asked.

"Well, it's true. Why should I think of such things? I am a soldier. Those other things are for the politicians." Kovacs was beginning to look dangerous. "Our job is to fight the war, not argue about it. A soldier is not supposed to get involved with politics."

"Why not?" Kane asked. "Who has more to lose than a soldier? We should be the first person concerned with politicians and what they decide."

"The President is elected. For us that is the end of it. After he is elected he is the Commander, and we must obey his orders."

The onlookers nodded in unison.

"Because we are soldiers, we must obey all orders—is that right, Hunky?—even if we know they are wrong?" Kane countered.

"You can't trap me, Kane. The book says 'Accomplish the mission.' If you feel the order is unlawful, then you protest later."

"That sure would be a big help if the order was to kill somebody," Bill shot back. "Did the goddamn book tell you how to get out of those rocks the other day?"

Kovacs started to sputter, "That's . . . that's different. I'm talking about Viet-Nam. If you don't like it, the next time there's an election you can vote."

"You're contradicting yourself," I pointed out. "First you say we're not supposed to think about politics and then you say we should vote. How can you vote intelligently if you don't think?"

"You're trying to twist me up again. I didn't say you shouldn't think when you vote," he shouted.

"Hunky," I replied. "You must have a very untroubled mind if you have to think only every four years."

"Not only that, Kovacs," Bill added. "If you follow that Commander-in-Chief routine to its ridiculous conclusion, you would have to vote for the President or be disloyal. Considering how many people are in the military, that's a lot of votes he would have sewed up."

"I'm not disloyal, but you two guys should be court-martialed for talking the way you do. If you don't like democracy you should go to some other country," he said, shaking his finger in livid fury.

"So you think Viet-Nam is a democracy, do you, Hunky?" I asked.

"You know goddamned well I'm not talking about

Viet-Nam, I'm talking about the United States. You act like you don't like the United States."

"That's just it, Kovacs—we do like it," Bill corrected. "But the day I'm court-martialed for expressing my opinion about it, I'll leave. The question is, are we helping our country by being here?"

"The people back home must think so—except for those screwed-up kids in school who should be reading their books instead of messing in things which are none of their concern. And besides the people back home re-elected the President," Kovacs finished.

"Well, first of all, Kovacs," I put in, "those screwed-up kids, as you call them, think it is their business because they're the ones who're going to be drafted. And unlike yourself they are thinking about politics . . ."

"Let me finish, Dunc," Bill said. "In the second place, Kovacs, you should know that the people at home don't know what they should about what is going on over here —what you know, if you'd stop and think. How can they really make a choice? In spite of that, they still voted against Goldwater because Johnson said he wanted out of Viet-Nam. Well, here we are, and I'm still asking, is it worth it?"

"Goddamit, Kane, I don't understand you. I expect shit like that from a nigger-lover like Duncan, but you —you're a soldier. What the hell are you trying to prove?"

Bill, grinning widely, turned to me and said, "I think that is a good place to rest our case, Reverend King. You and Hunky have parties to attend and . . ."

From the rear of the group there was some tittering and Vail, our Negro radio operator, asked in a loud voice, "Who ever said Martin Luther King was a nigger-lover?"

That did it. Everyone laughed, a bit louder than the remark merited, to push away the nervousness, and the tension was broken. Kovacs, confused, looked frustrated.

"Bill's right, Hunky. We better get going to the party. Coming, Grady?" I asked.

"Oh, I don't think so. I don't feel much like a party. You go without me. You can have my share of that Vietnamese chow."

"Listen, Grady," I said. "I could care less whether you eat or not, but I think you should be there. It could be your team soon and you had better establish some rapport before that happens."

Grady groaned, "I guess you're right, but I don't know if my poor old gut is up to it. Okay, I'll see you there as soon as I finish this drink."

Kane followed me out to the jeep.

"Why don't you come along to the party, Bill?" I grabbed the steering wheel and hauled myself in.

"Thanks, Dunc," he answered. "But I would only be in the way—it's a private thing."

"Well, can I give you a lift?"

"No, I have my own jeep."

"Tell me, Bill, those things you were saying to Kovacs in there . . ."

"Did I really mean them?" he finished for me. "I don't really know, I guess so . . ." He looked at the ground and kicked a stone.

"I've never heard you talk like that before—sounded like you've been doing some thinking."

Bill smiled through the gloom. "I don't speak often about things that don't have to do with my job for the same reason you use a lot of slang when you talk. We scare people when we speak straight—like Hunky."

"But what made you start thinking like this?"

"I don't know, Dunc. Like I said inside, this is my third trip here and I was pretty gung-ho. But this trip is different. The other two times, like most of us, I was always in a CIDG camp and met a lot of Montagnards. The only Vietnamese I really met were the LLDB,* and you know what a crummy bunch of bastards they are."

"I know what you mean. We really had to do a lot of weeding to find the men for these teams."

"That's just it, Dunc. All of a sudden I find there are good Vietnamese, and I worry about what is going to happen here. These guys on the team are good soldiers, but have you ever heard them talk about democracy, loyalty, patriotism, their government? The only loyalty they have is to this project and to us. They could care less about those bandits running things in Saigon. They're like lost souls."

"Have you ever talked to them quietly?"

"Not only them, but with other Vietnamese as well. Once they trust you, they sure don't say the things they're supposed to. Dunc, did you ever think that maybe there are worse things that could happen to this country than communism?"

I choked on my cigarette and almost fell from the jeep. "Like what?" The question rasped on my dry throat.

"Like nothing—or destroying it completely. It's getting worse. The Marines are here, the bombings are increasing, and the Regular Army will be here soon. The more we push, the more they fight back. Back in early sixty-four it looked like this war was almost over. I don't think either side was interested in fighting. But we fixed that, and we're in worse shape now than ever." He took a deep drag from his cigarette and ground it out.

"What do you mean, 'like nothing'?"

"Hell, you know the answer. These people have to do

* *Luc-Luong Dac-Biet*—Vietnamese Special Forces.

something. Their government isn't interested in them. It was bad when I first came here—now it's worse. Except for getting a lot of people killed, all we've accomplished is making some Saigon merchants richer and some province chiefs fatter."

"Sounds like you're saying we should let the VC have it."

"Christ, I don't know. The more I learn, the more screwed up the whole thing gets. Who the hell are the VC? I wouldn't want it, but then I'm not Vietnamese." He lit another cigarette.   ..

"Bill, you're the first guy I've ever heard talk like that over here—and of all people, a soldier with eighteen years' service."

Bill gave a little laugh, which sounded almost like embarrassment. "Maybe I never should have learned to read. Maybe they never should have sent me to Delta and allowed me to become exposed to so many non-military Vietnamese. Dunc, I know you don't have time now and we've both been drinking a little, but some night I'd like to sit down and talk this out."

I laughed and said, "Personally, I think you've already figured it out and are only looking for a sounding board. But I'd like to have that talk—any time. What the hell are you going to do?"

He took a deep breath before answering. "I don't know. I've got over half my life invested in the army. It's a helluva time to get disillusioned, with only two years to go. This will be my last trip over here. How about you —still thinking of getting out?"

I nodded. "I know why. Now all I have to do is to figure out how."

"I hope you make it, Dunc. Get out before it's too late. Just do me one favor—if you do get out, tell them about this place, tell both sides of the story. And tell them how the minds of people like Hunky work." He finished by jerking his thumb over his shoulder.

"It's a deal. But do you think you should be going out with the teams, feeling the way you do? There are enough things to worry about without having doubts on your mind."

"I've been thinking about that," he said seriously, then broke into a grin and tapped my shoulder with his fist. "Hell, I'm still a professional. I'll be okay. You better get to that party."

"Right"—I cranked the motor into action—"*Chao, trung si.*"

Bill stepped back—"*Chao, ong. Mai nhe*"—and crunched through the gravel to his jeep.

●　　●　　●

The man I have called Bill Kane never kept the appointment. The time never seemed right, and then, three weeks later, his team was ambushed. He was last seen carrying his wounded American partner over his shoulder, into the brush.

"They simply evolved a means of isolating every person emotionally from every other person, permitting each one to turn only to the system for guidance and friendship. This was, in its way, a brilliant maneuver. It solved the problem without the use of a single policeman by creating another kind of police force, a completely effective one that operates around the clock without a hitch and requires no salaries." *

EUGENE KINKEAD
In Every War But One

---

* *An explanation of how, by using "sinister" and devious means, the Chinese gained control over American prisoners of war in Korea.*

Fʀᴏᴍ ᴛʜᴇ ᴀʀᴍᴏʀʏ in Buffalo as a newly inducted draftee to the conversation in the bar in Viet-Nam spans ten and a half years. You have seen the beginning and the end of that decade, which I began as a Private (E-1) and ended as a Master Sergeant (E-8). Two months after my talk with Bill Kane, I received an Honorable Discharge, left the military womb, and returned to civilian life.

●   ●   ●

1954: the Korean "police action" was over, McCarthy had risen and fallen, people had heard of Dien Bien Phu but didn't know the location of Viet-Nam. French colonialism in Southeast Asia was finished, and the United States had taken the first fateful steps in Viet-Nam. The threat to the "free world" came from the Russian Bear in Europe.

1965: Berkeley sit-ins, Vietnam Day Committees, the Marines and Regular Army in Viet-Nam. (People now call Viet-Nam a war; the cost of war has risen sharply from a million dollars a day to a million dollars an hour.) Viet-Nam is talked of as if it were two countries: We no longer fight insurgents, we fight "invaders" from the

North. The threat to the "free world" is from the Chinese Dragon.

●　　●　　●

Staying in the Army beyond my two-year draft commitment makes me neither unique nor typical. I was nearly twenty-five when drafted, and nothing in the decade prior to that indicated that I would become a member of the Regular Army—a professional soldier.

I was raised in middle-class suburbia, and my father, a professional man, assumed I would go to college. But by the time I was a high school senior chafing under the regimentation of school and the restrictions imposed on and by a middle-class society, I could barely wait for my sixteenth birthday to quit school. When it came, I left school and got a job the same day.

I lived at home in an atmosphere of authority: there were rules, some explicit, some implied; there were certain standards of acceptable conduct. For many of these things there was neither logic nor reason; just an arbitrary "it's right or it's wrong" or "it just isn't done." Like many others, confused by these things and unable to define the contradictions, I lived with them and survived. There were inherent rewards for acceptance, self-destruction wasn't contemplated, we learned how to "make do." Oh, we broke rules, but the knowledge that they were rules and the awareness that we were breaking them only served to give them legitimacy. My parents were never to understand why I left school and home. But did I really leave? It is more accurate to say I took much of my sixteen-year home life with me into the world. We can no more leave those years at the doorstep than we can leave our years in the Army at the discharge center.

Starting with my first job, excluding an eight-month stint in an office, I invariably worked at things that kept me away from home and allowed me freedom of movement. When the employment became restrictive or confining, I quit and moved on. I worked as a lumberjack, tree topper, tree surgeon, foundryman, guide, trapper, park custodian, street worker, and garbageman. Some years the money was good, others, not so good. Sometimes I was low man, other times I was a foreman or supervisor. Places of employment stretched over thousands of miles and two countries.

I drank when and with whom I wanted to. Nobody told me when to get up or to go to bed. I took vacations when I wanted to and stayed until the mood moved me. I avoided clubs and organizations. In short, I led a very unregimented existence. I reveled in it and shunned anything that threatened it. I had enough contact with the military to know it was the antithesis of what I wanted from life. This wasn't a flight from responsibility—on the contrary, many of my jobs required conscious acceptance of responsibility. But the *1984* interpretation of the word was repugnant, and to accept it, I felt, would be to destroy my self, which would have been the ultimate irresponsibility.

These are the feelings and the simplistic philosophy I brought to Buffalo that day. A more unlikely candidate for membership in the world's largest and least democratic organization can hardly be imagined—yet I stayed.

I stayed in the U.S. Army for less simple reasons. If they must be reduced to one sentence it would have to be: I thought I was beating the system and making it work for me. The truth, of course, is just the opposite.

If my background is not unique (I admit it is not typical), neither is my failure to beat the military system.

Senator McCarthy had a field day while he was conjuring up bogeymen *for* the system, but when he turned his inferior firepower on the military, they annihilated him. The Congress and generations of tradition fought it out with the military after World War II and lost. Had they not lost, 27 December 1954 would have been nothing more for me than another work day. The military not only forced the idea of a large standing military on a people traditionally opposed to such an idea, but made them believe in its necessity. UMT * was voted in ostensibly to maintain freedom and American tradition when in fact it was designed by the military to perpetuate itself. Though this is contrary to tradition and the antithesis of freedom, it is now accepted without question.

Senator McCarthy, the Congress, the people—myself —underestimated the opposition, an organization employing more people, owning more land, controlling more money than any other organization in the world, reaching into every facet of our society, touching everybody and everything: the U.S. military.

I was trapped. Did those who served their two years and got out escape the trap? How many could see the contradiction in drafting people and then making them take the oath of enlistment? Most got out with an Honorable Discharge. They may have hated the two years of service, they may have disliked every professional soldier with whom they had contact. But they did not rebel, they compromised, adjusting to military ways and accepting the military's standards, and learning, if only to survive, how to think in military terms. They return to a society that for years has accepted military rationale to take jobs dependent directly or indirectly on military spending.

* Universal Military Training—the draft.

After two years of service the military maintains direct influence through the reserve obligation program.

Millions of words, unheeded by most, have been written about military power and control. Perhaps a look at the inner machinations and how they affected me and others might make the picture clearer.

"The common soldier, for example, carries out a whole series of functionally rational actions without having any idea as to the ultimate end of his actions or the functional role of each individual act within the framework of the whole."

KARL MANNHEIM

BASIC TRAINING does many things to men. Nobody remains unchanged by it. An analyst could write at the top of a piece of paper, "The Purpose of Basic Training Is:"—and go on to fill the page with a list that would include: instill discipline, learn how to work as a team, gain proficiency in weapons, create motivation, and so on. This is unnecessary verbiage, listing the means; one line would suffice to define the true end: "The purpose of basic training is to make each man a soldier, that is, an efficient killer."

I urge those who regard as intemperate the use of the word "killer" to define soldier to watch a basic training class in bayonet drill. Temperate? Watch as they learn to club and thrust, whirl and thrust again, each movement accompanied by guttural animal roars ripping from a hundred throats. What are they doing? They are learning to kill by the numbers in one of the most primitive and personal ways. The bonus teaching point? Aggressiveness wins. Don't wait for them—go get 'em! Before a trainee can graduate he must meet certain standards in marksmanship. The purpose of becoming an effective marksman is to make killing more efficient. The purpose of basic training is to train people to kill effectively, efficiently, and on command.

The severity, usually overrated, and the manner in which basic training is conducted varies from unit to unit and from service to service, but the purpose remains the same. Every man, whether he ends up as an infantry rifleman, a cook, a clerk, mechanic, or radar technician, must first learn the art and science of killing. The thousands of men who complete basic training each month are raised in a society giving at least lip service to "Thou shalt not kill." To make them an efficient part of an organization whose end purpose is to kill, certain fundamental steps are followed.

Each new recruit is subjected to a leveling process or depersonalization. While the hypothesis that all men are created equal may be valid, nobody suggests that "equal" means "same." We grow up in different neighborhoods in different homes with different parents. We go to different schools with different teachers. Education, both in and out of school, means different things to different people. At the end of our second decade, in spite of conforming to certain arbitrary rules of conduct, dress, and speech (varying according to locale, religion, social stratum, etc.), each of us has developed a set of values and is well on the way to forming a personal philosophy of life.

Before the military can impose its own peculiar and alien values on masses of men, it must first level all to a common base. It cannot erase the learned mechanical functions or the physical skills and dexterity gained; nor does it desire to do so. Rather, it endeavors to eliminate many of the individual's personal values so that his skills can be utilized by and for the military.

This reduction of the individual is done in a series of steps, each making the next one easier. The mass physical is one such step. It is true that due to "skinny dipping," school sports, communal showers, and so on, standing naked in a room with other naked men may be no novelty. But inspection of one's genital and rectal areas is something normally restricted to the privacy of a bathroom or the doctor's office, and milking one's penis in view of others is not an acceptable practice. To be obliged to do these in front of a hundred people leaves a feeling of debasement and contamination, and witnessing others' debasement adds to your own.

Having total strangers discuss your imperfections as if you were a piece of furniture or an automobile adds to the reduction. Men wear mustaches or comb their hair a certain way because they believe it looks better on them—it's a personal vanity, a mark of individualism. Both are removed, yet there is no written law in the Army stating that hair must be cut so short. It is an arbitrary rule, done in the name of sanitation and tradition. Few men get out of the barber's chair without feeling embarrassed and less than human, but for the cadre it has another feature: a "skinhead" is more likely to keep the unfamiliar hat on.

The closeness of barracks life, the continual lack of

privacy and forced social relationships (you are assigned bunkmates and a "buddy") are part of the process. Civilian clothes are packed and stored or shipped home, and now the men even look alike in their uniforms. Regardless of education or former social level, all are talked to in the same way and moved from place to place in large groups.

Outwardly, this seems to be a democratic process because it removes class consciousness. Actually it is a substitution, replacing one type of class consciousness for another. By being given a rank (recruit), you automatically belong to the lowest class. A corporal whom you have never seen and who may be less educated and less intelligent can give you orders. A Pfc. with an MP brassard can tell you how to stand or how to wear your hat. Stand at attention while talking to an NCO. Salute all officers; if a car has a blue bumper sticker (officer), salute it, regardless of who's driving.

Depersonalization can take place only if the subject is separated from normal references, that is, his social environment. This separation is both physical and symbolic, and the uniform, haircut, and new vocabulary are only part of it. Seldom does a trainee undergo training in a camp close to his home, and new trainees are not allowed passes. The military post is separated from the civilian populace, physically by fences and guards, and socially by its values, laws, and purpose for being. Prior to entering the military, men physically separate the three spheres of living—work, play, sleep. Now all aspects of life are conducted within the confines of the military post under one central authority.

The recruit's training is conducted according to a master plan emanating from a mysterious "on high." All daily activities—tightly scheduled and each leading at a prearranged time to the next—are carried on in the company of many others under the scrutiny of superiors. Control is maintained at all levels—Chain of Command —through a lack of communication and the hoarding of information. "Keeping the men informed" means giving them only that information necessary to get the job done —namely, that of making them soldiers. These enforced activities are brought together into a single rational plan designed to fulfill official aims.

The trainee is run from one strange environment to another to perform unfamiliar tasks, each of which creates feelings of confusion and uncertainty. Being educated is no protection and is often the opposite, giving rise to myths about idiot-geniuses and Ph.D.s who can't tie their shoelaces. Trainees are constantly sleepy even though they seldom sleep less than eight hours a night. I was no exception, yet before induction I had performed greater physical labor for longer periods of time, and eight hours of sleep had been a rarity. It certainly isn't the level of scholarship required that produces the fatigue. Army manuals are boring rather than challenging —"written by geniuses so idiots can understand them." This fatigue is part of the reorganization syndrome: depersonalized and disorganized, the trainee is ready for reorganization.

The recruit's first step in reorganization is to overcome confusion, which he does by learning the ropes— no matter how contradictory the dos and don'ts—and by finding out what he can and can't get away with. He is presented with a new set of regulations and house rules and strange requirements of conduct, all explained in the Uniform Code of Military Justice and the Manual for Courts-Martial. The process boils down to learning "Do those things that please the cadre. His superiors will be happy and you'll stay out of trouble."

Actions which at worst would be considered bad manners in a civilian are now punishable crimes. If he quits this job and goes home, he's a deserter; if he convinces others to strike against conditions, he's guilty of conspiracy and mutiny. He is now in a society where everyone does what is required, under conditions in which one infraction stands out against the constantly examined compliance of the others. Non-existent in this society are habeas corpus, the right to be tried by a jury of peers, or bail. Stripped of all past supports, he is prepared to start living by "the book," thereby becoming a soldier.

The trainee now tries to anticipate the cadre, to "keep him off my back," and the rationale is, "If I do everything right without being told, I won't be singled out for reprimand and Sarge won't remember my name when a shitty detail comes along, or he'll remember my name because of my efforts and will reward me by not picking me for shitty details." The results are the same whatever the reasoning—the trainee does what is expected with a minimum of supervision.

Recruits regard most of their training cadre as not too bright or just plain bastards, and the arbitrary rules as senseless. Yet with rare exceptions they end up emulating the cadre and obeying the rules.

The recruit has now learned how the system works and how he can work within its confines. He believes he can make it work for him, in other words, beat the system by utilizing the new-found reward-punishment system. To rebel against the injustice, arbitrariness, or the senselessness of an order will result in trouble and more orders. A surfeit of orders means confusion; the fewer the orders, the less the confusion and the easier it is to comply, and compliance means being able to have a beer at the PX or a longer smoke break. The way to beat the system is to excel in it—perhaps you will become a trainee squad leader, exempt from KP—supervising details, not performing them—and life will be easier. Or perhaps you will become a trainee platoon sergeant and supervise the squad leaders and march beside the platoon rather than in it. Since those who want your privileges are working harder at learning to replace you, you will have to work to stay ahead. Individual acts can result in the withdrawal of privileges for the group, so the group exhorts the individual to shape up . . . or else.

Natural desires for individuality and recognition become manipulatory tools. One way to achieve a degree of individuality and recognition is to be the eight ball or screw-up, which will mean additional harassment and drawing all the bad details, and worse, the disapproval and possible ostracism by your buddies. The other way is to excel at one thing or at many things within the system: be the one who always has well-pressed fatigues, the cleanest rifle, the best spit-polished boots, the tightest bunk, the neatest foot locker. This results in recognition, which even the worst recruit craves; give him a taste of it and he will strive for more. The result of striving for individuality is mass conformity to official standards.

No, of course I didn't realize these things were happening—and even if I had, what could I have done about it? There are only two alternatives—the stockade or over-the-hill, and our society cooperates so well with the military that the future is grim for the man with an Undesirable Discharge. But there was no problem: I finished as a squad leader. Like the others, I saw nothing incongruous in six men sitting on as many toilets after lights-out, swapping rumors, shining boots, having a bowel movement, eating ice cream, or finishing a pocket book—the same men who were embarrassed during a physical a few short weeks earlier. We had a new vocabulary and affected various degrees of Southern accents.

The weeks ahead would be taken up with Advanced Individual Training, Basic Unit Training, and Advanced Unit Training. For some this meant learning to be radio operators, cooks, mechanics, and clerks. For most it would be a refinement of basic training and learning other ways to kill. Throughout, of course, there would be the usual TI and E lectures, mostly about the virtues of NATO and the Russian menace, why it was essential for us to go to Germany, how important we were to the defense of Europe. (The situation was so dangerous that some units arrived in Germany having never spent four consecutive days on bivouac in the field—canceled because of bad weather.)

Having made up my mind that the army could be bearable if not for work like guard, KP, and police call, I took the bait and endeavored to get promoted, which involved my working harder than those around me. Within a year I had a corporal's rating; in my twenty-seven months in Germany I was promoted four times. Life in Germany was pleasant, with enough field work to break the monotony, and I achieved the recognition I felt I needed. I became a well-trained soldier.

After Germany it was Fort Hood, Texas, giving basic training instead of taking it, first as a cadreman and then as the company training NCO, and finally building my first personal empire—a training aids center—and glowing from the pat on the head that comes from "getting the job done." Next to Fort Bliss, Texas, and another empire—re-enlistment NCO, training NCO, battalion operations sergeant.

In short, the years were to be interesting to me, boring to you, and non-productive to us both. This was a time to gather anecdotes for lulls in conversation at company parties and a time filled with the little rewards that keep a person feeling he is productive. For a soldier it was to be a productive six years, for an individual it would be stagnation, a limbo. I would love it—I was an organization man.

•　　•　　•

At the end of eight weeks, trainees are no longer confused, don't feel the need for as much sleep, and have forgotten their reason for griping. In spite of "stupid" cadre and "senseless" instructions, they have done what was planned for them. They are now soldiers—they know how to kill on command.

THIS IS NOT an indictment of the U.S. Army's methods of conducting basic training. Although refinements and minor variations are possible, this is the way a soldier is created. That this metamorphosis can be accomplished in eight weeks or less without employing physical abuse or hypnosis is a testament to the efficiency of the total organization. The fundamental principles—depersonalization, isolation, reorganization—are not unique to the United State military. The Army of any country utilizes these techniques; to do otherwise would risk having an ineffective, unresponsive force.

All nations regard the maintenance of an army as necessary to "protect the national interests," whether threats to them are real, imagined, or invented. An army can fulfill its purpose only if it has the capacity and the will to kill. To accept the basic premise, the people of a nation must accept in their midst a force trained to kill effectively and on command.

Because the military man's values differ from those of the civilian community, his approach to problems and his thinking are different from the civilian's. Many see a danger in this separation of communities and the difference in thinking, but the danger is in the breach. If the civilian community has absolute control over the military counter-community, the separation and difference are healthy; if control is to be maintained, separation and difference are essential. Do we in this country have these essentials?

A civilian community can control the counter-community through money (matériel) or manpower (size). For these controls to be realized, two conditions must be met: the military establishment must have a set minimum strength—determined by the civilian community on the basis of population rather than gross national product—except in time of war or *real* national emergency; pay and allowances should be high enough to make soldiering in all ranks attractive as a career—to prevent a large manpower turnover, monetary gain must be high enough to offset the more unattractive features of army life.

Thousands of young men annually are drafted; threatened with the draft, thousands more enlist to take advantage of options offered to encourage such action. Whether two-year draftees or three- or four-year enlistees, the vast majority get out when their hitch is completed. This brings us back to the original question: By getting out, did they escape the trap? The answer is no!

With rare exceptions these men earned an Honorable Discharge * and most received Good Conduct Medals. They weren't court-martialed, they didn't go to jail, and many were promoted from E-1 to E-4 or E-5. In their opinion they beat the system.

Very few of the thousands were ever ordered to kill but all were trained to kill, in the process accepting the military values, becoming participants in the military reward-punishment system, accepting and carrying out

* Or an Honorable Discharge conditional on their fulfilling their reserve obligation.

the military's solution to problems. They learned to understand military thinking and thought in those terms for two, three, or four years. In short, military reorganization "took." It matters little that they may have detested those years because, as planned, they did everything that the military expected of them.

Each year thousands become part of the counter-community; each year thousands return to the civilian community. This cycle has continued for twenty-five years in the United States with only one short break. The number of men who have returned with Honorable Discharges testifying to their reorganization now is in the millions, and they have brought with them their ability to think in military terms.

They have returned to suburbia and tract housing. They belong to the Rotary, the Lions, the Masons, the Legion, and to every church. They are mechanics, junior executives, journalists, corporation directors, city councilmen, state assemblymen, and Congressmen. They marry and raise children who in turn will enter the military. Most become "solid citizens" in the community; they *are* the community—they set the standards.

They either are or help elect the men who vote the money for the military. They work for, are the head of, or profit from military contracts passed out to civilian companies. Generals who justify military needs retire one day and become corporate board chairmen the next. The corporations readily see the necessity for a large standing army and Universal Military Training. It becomes easier each year to sell the civilian community on the "real" dangers to the United States, and we find ourselves increasingly backing military solutions to what are basically political problems.

We still had a safety margin from 1945 through 1947

when the military used its large officer corps, its propaganda machinery and techniques gained during the war, hired Madison Avenue publicists, produced films, and built its UMT model at Fort Knox—all at taxpayers' expense—to sell the necessity for a large standing army and UMT. Danger was imminent, we were told; we were in a state of national emergency, and to oppose the military solution could only be a subversive act that could end in democracy's destruction. Traditionally, it is the role of the people to declare through the Congress what constitutes a national emergency and to tell the military what it should do. The military, that most undemocratic of all institutions, was telling the people what was good for democracy.

Much to the consternation of the military, UMT was turned down by the Congress. The military scare campaign slipped into high gear, UMT was billed as our only insurance against extinction, and six months later they got their way. (That day we began losing our safety margin.) From the 1947 struggle against UMT we have progressed to accepting it as an everyday part of American life.

The saturation of the civilian community by men accustomed to thinking in military terms has been so pervasive that we have lost the essentials necessary for absolute civilian control. Within the United States today, for all practical purposes, there is no separation of the communities and no difference in thinking. We have, in fact, military thinking in civilian clothing.

Reorganized society elects governments that perpetuate and strengthen the military establishment and give it money on military recommendation. Since the military reorganizes more people, the perpetuation of a society that will elect such governments is assured. The money given the military is channeled back to the people to manufacture matériel for the military. By maintaining the structure and illusion of democracy but not its function, we have established the perfect military state. There is no longer a counter-community: we have evolved into a single militaristic community.

Small wonder that the nation can accept the rationale "We make war to make peace; our commitments in Viet-Nam and other places are designed to prevent our becoming involved in a war; we are in Viet-Nam to protect the Vietnamese from the Vietnamese invaders." The wonder is that we aren't involved simultaneously in thirty Vietnams.

Meaningful debate and a serious search for alternatives are fast becoming extinct. The essential difference between the Democratic and the Republican Party approaches to Viet-Nam is that one says we should do more and the other says we are doing enough while continuing to do more. The whole nation is playing the military "Yes, but . . ." game: "Yes, I know the war is a terrible thing and taxes are high, but . . ." Congress has become the military's fund raiser and the President a social worker to pacify the people.

How far we've come! The conservative elements in the United States, who in the past have been the advocates of isolationism, restriction of the military, suppression of socialism, and a return to the basic American traditions, are today the greatest advocates of the necessity for protecting "our interests" around the world and the most ardent military boosters—the largest single example of total socialism featuring all the worst aspects of such an ideology. Those who resist what we have become and wish for a return to basic traditions are called subversive.

Donald Duncan

Do those who get out of service after their two-, three-, or four-year hitch escape the trap? No—they perpetuate it.

● ● ●

"... a standing army, however necessary it may be at sometimes, is always dangerous to the liberties of the people. Soldiers are apt to consider themselves as a body distinct from the rest of the citizens. They have their arms always in their hands. Their rules and their discipline are severe. They soon become attached to their officers and disposed to yield implicit obedience to their commands. Such a power should be watched with a jealous eye."

SAMUEL ADAMS, 1776

IV

"*That the people and the States should, for a sufficient period of time, elect an uninterrupted succession of men ready to betray both; that the traitors should throughout this period, uniformly and systematically pursue some fixed plan for the extension of the military establishment; that the governments and the people of the States should silently and patiently behold the gathering storm, and continue to supply the materials, until it should be prepared to burst on their own heads, must appear to every one more like the incoherent dreams of a delirious jealousy, or the misjudged exaggerations of a counterfeit zeal, than like the sober apprehensions of genuine patriotism.*"

JAMES MADISON
The Federalist XLVI

Don," my wife calls from the front door, "there's a phone call for you."

I mutter "damn," shove the large suitcase in place, and back out of the station wagon. In the air-conditioned coolness of the frame house I ask, "Who is it?"

"I don't know. Maybe your office. I'll have the ice chest packed by the time you're finished talking."

Why the hell is the office phoning? They know I'm on leave. I bark, "Hullo. Duncan speaking."

"This is Colonel Wagell, Adjutant General's Office, Fourth Army Headquarters . . ."

"Okay, Manelli, knock it off, I'm in the middle of packing the car. If you're calling to ask about a golf game, I'm leaving for Las Vegas in one hour."

"Is this Sergeant First Class Donald W. Duncan of the 59th Artillery?"

"Come on, Manelli, I don't have time to play games."

"*Sergeant!*" The explosion has enough authority to draw me to attention. "This *is* the Fourth Army Adjutant General." Sounds real, but unknown colonels don't call sergeants long distance at their private quarters. "Do you have an application asking for assignment to Special Forces?"

I hesitate. "Ye-es. I did put in an application back in

January or February, along with a Sergeant Mott. He has left, so I assume my application is disapproved."

"Are you still interested in the assignment?"

"Yes"—Manelli, if this is your idea of a joke, I'll throttle you for making a fool of me—"sir."

"We can approve the assignment, providing you agree to certain conditions. You must cancel your leave and start immediately. You will have to waive your right to proficiency pay." (Ouch!) "Special Forces cannot utilize your MOS * and since the assignment is voluntary, you are not entitled to the money. You will go PCS † but TDPFO . . ."

"Uh, what's that?"

"Temporary duty pending further orders. You will be permanently transferred but will not be able to move your family until training is completed and you have a permanent assignment to a unit. You understand that if you fail to complete jump school and are not drawing pro-pay, you can be assigned anywhere, regardless of MOS?"

"Yes, sir, I agree to all that."

"You do? Are you sure you fully understand everything I've said?"

"Yes, sir."

"All right, the application is approved. You report to Fort Bragg, North Carolina, tomorrow."

"How?" The bastards are doing everything to discourage me. They've had that application for weeks and didn't have to wait until now.

"What do you mean?"

"This is El Paso, Texas. Regulations prevent me from driving such a distance in twenty-four hours, and it would

* Military Occupational Specialty.
† Permanent Change of Station.

be impossible anyway. I have no orders authorizing air travel—for that matter, I have no orders authorizing me to clear this installation."

"Mmm. Yes, of course . . . is a problem. If we make the arrangements, can you be ready to leave on a plane first thing in the morning?"

"Yes, sir."

"We'll make the arrangements. We'll give Post Headquarters verbal authority to cut orders with a fund citation authorizing air travel. You start clearing immediately."

Waaahooo! I leap from the couch. My wife runs in from the kitchen.

"What is it?"

"I've been accepted for Special Forces. I leave tomorrow morning by plane!" I almost dance with excitement as I give Loni the details.

"But what about our trip to Las Vegas and California? It's the first vacation we've had." I am alone in my enthusiasm.

"What's a two-week vacation? This is a whole new career! To hell with the leave."

"But the money—you lose pro-pay and have to give up your part-time job with the detective agency, and you'll lose your separate ration money. How long will you be gone? How long is the training? Why didn't you tell them no?"

"Are you kidding? After all the trouble I went through to get accepted? After spending months getting the information for my security clearance, after all that exercising and dieting? After three years of putting up with the boredom and frustration of garrison duty, working at inventing work, playing petty politics, making up phony training schedules, putting on worthless demonstrations for VIPs, you want me to turn down a chance to get with an organization that is really doing something—a chance to be with the best instead of these homesteaders? I'm going. I'd leave today if I had to!"

IN THE SMALL Fayetteville, North Carolina, airport the humidity makes my TWs * feel like a hair-lined cellophane bag. The post taxi hurries past ugly signboards, neon lights, a jungle of car lots, pawnshops, trailer camps, small shops, and onto the post. It stops in front of the headquarters of the U.S. Army's Seventh Special Forces Group. Orders checked, I am directed to a half-empty barracks, where I stow gear, make the bed, and change into cool civilian clothing.

Outside, the rows of wooden barracks surrounded by pine trees contrast sharply with the treeless sterility of Fort Bliss with its modern air-conditioned buildings. Small groups of talking men barely glance my way, but as I start to pass the fourth barracks, a familiar voice halts me.

"Dunc, you made it!" Ted Mott's short stocky frame moves through the group sitting on the steps, and we shake hands. His round, sunburned Irish face is all grins. "I had given you up, Dunc. When did you get in? How did you get them to turn you loose? Where are you living? What . . ."

"Whoa," I laugh, "one at a time." I try to tell him of the phone call and my hectic departure from Fort

* Tropical Worsted uniform.

Bliss. "How about you? How long have you been here?"

"Three days. I took a thirty-day leave before I showed up. Got drunk, almost got married. But that can wait. Let me introduce you to some people. Jack, Earl, Ed . . . this is the guy from Fort Bliss I was telling you about. He's a 'leg' but he's trying to go honest."

The last is a reference to my being a non-jumper, and for the first time I notice that each man wears cloth Airborne wings over the left pocket of his fatigues. They shake hands readily enough, but I feel they are lowering themselves for Ted's sake because of my "leg" status—I'm not in the club.

"Dunc," Ted continued, "you'll love this place. They've got an NCO club here you won't believe. In fact, go back and get a coat and tie and meet me back here. We'll go and eat, and you can tell me what happened to McDougall and Handy. I'll be showered when you get back. Bring a copy of your orders so you can get a membership card."

He hadn't lied about the club. Barber shop, liquor store, stag bar, bar-lounge, TV room, swimming pool, terrace, huge ballroom, and large dining room; Ted said it had cost more than a million dollars. Two gin and tonics, a thick steak on a sizzling platter and a salad served by a shapely waitress—and the world looked beautiful. I filled Ted in on his friends at Fort Bliss and he supplied me with the details of his one-month romance. A year or two younger than I, Ted, as usual, talked and gesticulated like an enthusiastic teen-ager, an effect heightened by his burnt cheeks, peeling nose, and close-cut sun-bleached hair. In three days he seemed to have met everybody in the club.

After coffee we move to the lounge where we can look down on the ballroom through the separating glass.

It is cool and quiet, and the deep leather chairs cradle us while we drink.

"Still in shape for jump school, Dunc?"

"Well, after you left, things looked pretty hopeless so I fell off my diet and stopped running . . . I feel pretty good."

"I hope so," he grins. "It's going to be rough but you have a week before you start so you should make it."

"A week? You mean I can't get started for a week?" I can't hide my disappointment and impatience.

"Before Special Forces will let you go over to the 82nd school, you have to pass a PT test. You'll be under a Master Sergeant Craft for that week, and I don't envy you. He'll run you to death. If you pass by him, jump school won't be a problem physically."

"Tell me about the training. What can I expect?"

"It's mostly harassment—everything by the numbers, everything on the double. You'll find yourself in the push-up position more than vertical. Everything you do will be wrong which means more push-ups and squat jumps. Learning the equipment and how to jump is the easy part. The jump tower won't bother an old tree climber like you. It's the harassment. They try to make you lose your temper and quit. As an NCO you'll probably get a little extra dose of harassment—or maybe it only seems that way, because an NCO or officer is out of the habit of being on the receiving end."

"What's the purpose? Sounds like a bunch of unnecessary crap to me. Why don't they teach you to jump and let it go at that?"

Ted laughs. "Well, as they put it, 'To make you mentally alert and physically fit.' For instance they have a game called 'Hit It.' One of the cadre yells 'hit it,' maybe as you're running somewhere, and you come down stiff-legged on both heels, knees locked. You bend at the waist, head down and looking at your boots, with elbows locked at your side. Forearms are stretched out with the fingers spread as if wrapped around a reserve chute. That's all done in a single motion and before your heels hit you start yelling as loud as possible, 'one thousand, two thousand, three thousand, four thousand.' You immediately straighten up, reach overhead with your arms, bend back your head and stare straight up at the sky. You stand like that until the cadre says 'Recover.' Then you sound off with 'Clear, Sergeant!' and slap your legs with open palms and start off running again. If you don't react quickly enough or do it wrong, it costs you push-ups—and if those aren't correct you'll get more. If you're wearing equipment, you do squat jumps instead. They tell you to do ten, you give them one extra and shout 'One for Airborne!' Don't shout loud enough and it's more push-ups."

"You mean to say grown men go through that routine in front of the whole world? I'll feel like an ass."

"You'd better get used to it. If you don't you'll end up with very sore muscles. At the end of two weeks you'll be doing it so automatically that if you were on that dance floor and I yelled 'hit it,' you'd do it. The stiff-legged, bent-over position is the approved manner for exiting aircraft. The counting is the number of seconds it takes for your chute to open, and you reach up and look to check. It's a nice thing to know."

"And if it isn't?"

"It's reserve time. The theory in jump school is that everybody is scared to jump from a plane. So when you stand in the door and the jumpmaster says 'hit it' or 'go,' you'll be on your three-thousand count before you realize you no longer have an airplane under you. Another theory is, if you do enough push-ups and squat jumps, your muscles will get so tired and sore they start sending little messages saying, 'Jack, you better get on the ball 'cause we'uns down here is getting plumb pooped!' "

"Some alertness," I laugh. "You get so alert your brain no longer thinks, it only reacts. Sounds like brainwashing. But I'm thirty years old, not some eighteen- or nineteen-year-old kid. It just won't take at my age."

"We'll see," says Ted as a tall, expensively dressed man approaches our table.

"Hello, Ted. Mind if I sit down for a drink?"

"Jack McCallister, Don Duncan. Jack is a team sergeant in the Seventh."

Jack, sitting with the ease of one accustomed to his surroundings, modestly accepts Ted's overt respect as his due. The tan of his hawkish face is well set off by an immaculate white shirt. When another round of drinks appears, he waves aside our protests and pays the tab from a large roll of bills.

"Dunc is getting ready to start jump school and I was telling him what to expect."

With impressionable me as audience the two start playing "I remember when." Tales of excruciating exercise, jump cadre, jumps—all involving hilarious mishaps —all prove that paratroopers are a wonderfully special breed of cat and that I'm still not in the club. After thirty minutes of this Jack sees the girl he is expecting and excuses himself.

Ted leans forward conspiratorially and whispers, "He just brought his team back from a mission. See that roll he had on him?"

I'm puzzled. "Mission? What kind of mission? You mean a field training exercise?"

Ted, looking dramatically over his shoulder, stage whispers, "I mean a *real* mission. He's been gone six months."

Ted intercepts more questions with a furtive wave-off, and I am left to my own imagination. I feel a visceral thrill. Here's an outfit that's really doing something. My mind conjures clandestine operations.

When Ted assures me that tomorrow will be mostly processing, we continue to drink. Already a paratrooper, Ted will start his Special Forces training immediately. He has been selected for O and I, Operations and Intelligence, and has already received a schedule of subjects: Tactical Terrain Analysis, Fingerprinting, Order of Battle, Operational Planning, Photography, Cryptography, Clandestine Communications, Intelligence Nets, Methods of Interrogation, Organizing Guerrilla Units, Psychological Warfare. My own qualms make Ted's casual reference to them very impressive. Some of the titles leave the subject matter a complete mystery.

I think of my farewell from Fort Bliss and the envious and admiring eyes of those I was leaving. These men are really "Special." Am I over my head? Can I make it? I must make it.

As a WHISTLE SWELLS in my head and clamors for release, I find myself staring at a bare lightbulb. The resulting agony can only be because of the electrodes of the light being attached directly to my eyes. The walls vibrate with the sound of a man's voice crowding against the whistle inside my head. Why can the sound get in but not out? The explosion point is very near.

"Be out in the street in two minutes. Uniform: T-shirt, athletic shorts, and combat boots."

You must be kidding—nobody wears a uniform like that. My eyes make the agonizing turn to the voice. The voice isn't kidding—that's what he's wearing. Small head, bronze skin, cigar clamped between teeth, smooth muscular legs, massive chest. On him it doesn't look silly, it looks frightening. Stenciled on the T-shirt is M/SGT CRAFT.

No time to wash or brush the crud off my tongue and teeth, but I manage not to be the last one on the street. Ted, you son of a bitch. My watch says 4:30.

● ● ●

We run. This whole place must be built on a hill. Nobody runs this long without a break. I'm soaking wet, my combat boots feel like diver's boots, my watch weighs five pounds. We run. My throat wheezes and rasps trying futilely to pass air to my starved lungs, I can't lift my arms. We run. My legs belong to somebody else, everything blurs, the voice runs back and forth exhorting us to close up, stay in step, don't lag—when does he breathe? We run. My gut cramps, I stumble, my mind is mush, I have to breathe again. The T-shirt in front of me stops and I run into it. Happiness is being able to shoot that voice. It's over. What a helluva way to get rid of excess alcohol.

I manage to rubberleg it into the barracks. It takes five minutes for my breathing to return to normal. A man says we ran eight miles. Eight miles! Only the knowledge that if I don't move to the shower now I'll never move again gets me off the bunk.

Whether it was the run or the huge breakfast, my hangover is gone. Not a bad idea, I reflect—PT before the sun comes up and it's still relatively cool. The next two hours are spent in cleaning the barracks, police call, and meeting the other "trainees," NCOs all. Master Sergeant Reed—stocky, about my height but thicker and with a bull neck, about my age—is appointed barracks leader. He gives the impression of quick intelligence but it could be experience. The only thing bothering me about him is that I have the vague feeling he enjoyed the early run. Only Master Sergeant Brulet—older than either of us, with a sensitive face and wearing glasses—resents Reed's appointment. He has the apparent shrewdness of a "make-out artist" but my opinion is colored by his having spent the last couple of years as a civilian recruiter. I can't remember seeing him until well after the run.

We lounge in the shade, escaping the already intense heat, swapping lies, and speculating on when we'll be able to start training. When Craft appears and directs Reed to have everyone in athletic shorts and ready for PT in five minutes, my breakfast becomes a heavy lump of indigestible dough in my stomach.

Sweat-soaked before we complete the short jog to the parade field, for two hours we do endless repetitions of the "daily dozen" with some of Craft's personal innovations. Only the fact I am in a rear rank where I can fudge allows my legs to survive twenty squat jumps. Finally we assemble and I look forward to the showers and . . . my God, what's he doing? He's pointing us the wrong way. We run.

Reason tells me that a circular course must have as many downs as ups but my lungs and legs know better. My dry throat rasps, I can't count cadence—even if I had the air, the words could never squeeze past my swollen tongue—my feet seem to flap against the hot asphalt of the road. And always the voice of Craft exhorting us to greater effort.

We stop running and walk down one of the rare parts of this road-turned-racetrack that slopes down. At the bottom we resume running—uphill. Craft has a variation. Run one mile, walk one minute, and always resume running on an uphill portion. Hang on, go to the next block, make it to the walking point. When is the madman going to stop? The fourth lap—maybe he'll stop on this one. I can't keep in step. Reed, looking as fresh as when he started, sounds off loud and clear. He *is* enjoying it. Bastard. We are walking down the slope again, just in time. Oh, Christ! I can't hold it. My stomach cramps and I spew my breakfast alongside the road.

"Don't fall out, just puke, keep walking." The voice again. I'll kill him. We run. My nostrils are burning, I can barely see through the tears. He has to stop this time

Donald Duncan

around. The voice is coming from miles away. Someone
steps on my heels, I almost go down. The incline seems
to go straight up. My face must be only inches from the
black top. I have to stop at the next barracks. A little
further. It's over. Six laps—six miles.

I heave and tremble and one leg twitches. Craft is
talking. My vision clears a little. I don't believe it. He
isn't even breathing hard; in fact, he is barely sweating.
I catch the last part: ". . . and don't eat a heavy lunch.
All those who finished the run will take a PT test at
1330 hours. Those passing will start jump school next
Monday." A what? I notice for the first time that only a
third of the group is left.

Because we are checked individually there is time for
rest between each portion of the test. I pass the exercises
but the squat jumps take everything left in my legs. I
worry about the four-mile run.

I have reason to worry. After one lap my legs are
almost without coordination. No matter how hard my
lungs work and how hard my heart beats, I can't get
oxygen and blood to the muscles and joints. Almost three
laps. The next rise is ahead. If I can just make that. I'm
floating. I can't feel anything. I'm conscious only of the
roaring in my ears. What's that black mass rushing
toward me? I stick out my arms to ward it off. Pain. My
palms, my wrists, my head. I look around. It's strangely
silent on the road. My legs have betrayed me; I have
failed.

DOUBLE TIME! Double time! I feel as if I've been running my entire life without really learning how. Now it's up the wooden stairs to the top of the thirty-four-foot tower. The parachute harness straps bind my legs and pinch my shoulders, and the dummy reserve chute hanging on my front straps keeps hitting my knees. I wish the four men ahead of me would slow down on the stairs so I could. At the top of the tower the first man enters a box that simulates an aircraft fuselage. I wait on the steps, a riser in each hand. Instead of running from the back straps to a canopy, the risers terminate at spring snap-fasteners. I move up the two steps and can see into the large box with two doors leading out to the thirty-four-foot step. A man disappears out one door; another starts to move to the opposite door.

Inside. I stare at the back of the man in front as the jumpmaster leans outside and pulls in two straps, each ending in a steel ring. Out of sight, the other ends are attached to a trolley on a cable. The jumpmaster slams the rings onto the snaps held in the man's outstretched hands.

"Stand in the door!" The voice is overly loud. As soon as the man reaches and turns into the door he yells, "Roster number!"

The jumper hesitates and finally replies, "Roster Number Six, Sergeant."

"Hit it!"

The body in the door jerks forward involuntarily. At the last possible second hands clutch at the sides of the door. He doesn't go.

"Stand back from the door, Roster Number Six. Number Six, do you want to be a paratrooper?" A mute nod. "The only way that is going to happen, Number Six, is if you jump." The jumpmaster isn't yelling. He's actually counseling in a quiet, even voice, looking straight into the face of the man in the harness. "You can't get hurt, Number Six. There is absolutely no way you can hit the ground. The equipment is safe. You want to do it, don't you? Good. Stand in the door. Hit it!"

The same involuntary jerk. He whispers, "I can't, I can't," pleading for someone to push him.

The jumpmaster grabs the risers and jerks the man from the door. He puts his face close and yells, "You're a leg. A leg quitter. You look like a leg and you smell like a leg. You'll always be a leg and you'll always be a quitter. No guts. Get out of here before your leg smell stinks up my tower—and take off that equipment. That's a man's equipment and you're not fit to wear it. Get out!"

The man is in tears. Each sentence of the attack has landed on him like a flaying chain.

The jumpmaster whirls on me. "Are you going to jump, Roster Twelve?"

"Yes, Sergeant." I'd jump without the risers into burning oil after that scene.

He snaps on the rings and yanks the risers from my hand. "Stand in the door!"

I shuffle forward and turn into the door until the toe of my right boot is outside. My palms press hard against the outside of the shack. Knees slightly bent, my left foot ready to push, I glance down. I see the scorer sitting on his high perch, book open, ready for my jump. A man to the left is doing push-ups.

"Roster Number!"

"Roster Number Twelve, Sergeant," I bellow.

"Hit it!"

Push up and out. Feet together . . . "One thousand . . ." elbows in, hands on the reserve, knees stiff . . . "Two thousand . . ." I'm looking past the toes of my boots at the scorer—Christ! I'm going to land in his lap . . . "Three thousand . . ." My chin digs into my chest; the reserve hits my lip; straps dig into my groin. I'm going up—now back down. The ground is sliding past —I'm riding. Reach up and grab the risers. Did I say four thousand? I look down again, the ground blurs slightly as I pick up speed on the sloping cable. Just in time I remember to pull on the risers and lift my feet and the red dirt mound rushes by. The rubber bungy hits the risers and I swing back to the mound. A pair of hands stop my flight and unhook me.

"How was it, Dunc?" It's Brulet. It's over. I had made my first tower jump. I was now a "trolley trooper."

"Great!" I run off the mound back to the high chair to get my score. Up the tower, out the door, back to the mound. I feel like a veteran. Back to the high chair. I stare up at the scorer until he looks at me. Feet together, slap my sides, "Roster Number Twelve, Sergeant."

"Satisfactory jump, Twelve." I'm elated. "Take off your equipment and report back to the sergeant on my left." I'm disappointed; everyone else is jumping three or four times.

"Yes, Sergeant." Slap my sides and start to double time.

Donald Duncan

"Roster Number Twelve!" Freeze. "The proper answer is 'Clear, Sergeant.' Get ten."

I fall to the front leaning rest and count off ten push-ups and one for Airborne. Spring to my feet.

"You failed to say 'Clear, Sergeant' when I told you the proper answer. Ten more."

"Clear, Sergeant." I snap my sides and count them off. Back on my feet.

"Roster Twelve, you are wearing equipment. When wearing equipment, you do squat jumps, not push-ups. Get ten."

"Clear, Sergeant." The reserve parachute makes it almost impossible to retain balance. Back at attention.

"That was for the first mistake, Roster Twelve. Give me ten for the second."

"Clear, Sergeant." Christ. My knees can't take much more of this.

"You made a third mistake when you did the wrong exercise. Ten more."

"Clear, Sergeant."

The man is a sadist. I barely make it back to my feet. I wait expectantly. He turns back to me. "What are you doing, Number Twelve? I told you to take off your equipment. Give me ten for being stupid and get on with it."

"Clear, Sergeant." Slap my sides. Up and down eleven more times. On my feet, slap my sides and double time away chanting, "Airborne, Airborne . . ."

It's a relief to get out of my harness and put it on someone else. I start back to the scorer's seat but not before I do ten push-ups for a button that has been ripped from my fatigues by the harness. I chant my way back to the sergeant standing beside the scorer.

"Roster Number Twelve, where have you been? You're too slow. Get ten."

I am barely back on my feet when I'm back pushing for the unbuttoned pocket.

"Now get that line and relieve the man on the inside trolley."

"Clear, Sergeant."

Another trainee hands over a coiled line with a hook on the end. I run toward the mound and pass the man I am to relieve running toward the tower pulling a trolley. At the mound I throw one end of the line to the man on top and stand at parade rest. The trolley with the jumper attached passes over my head. The mound man unhooks him and hooks my end of the line to the trolley rings. I run back to the tower dragging the trolley on its uphill cable. Damn, it's heavy!

Three other pullers are waiting to take their trolley in. I look at the tower and the jumpmaster waves me in. To make sure it gets in the door, I have to pick up speed and I almost run into the tower. As soon as I stop, another line is put in my hand. Back to the mound. It looks three football fields away. The sun tries to push me into the dust. I'm getting hotter and sweating less—must be two hours since I've had a drink. I reach the mound in a dead heat with the trolley. Back to the tower—race the trolley to the mound. When will I get a break? That bastard on the next line is dogging—I've made three trips to his two. Back again. I'm no longer sweating; the 105° heat is telling. Almost an hour now. "Bring it in, Twelve . . . Hurry up, Twelve." Why don't I quit? I feel light-headed in spite of my fifty-pound helmet. The mound again. If I can make it back to the tower, I'll quit.

"Roster Number Twelve, where have you been? You're slowing down."

I look past the cadre on the top of the mound and

fight to control my face so hatred doesn't show. Never let your face show what you think—can get gigged for thinking improperly.

"You want a rest, Number Twelve?"

"Yes, Sergeant." Was that croak me?

"Okay, Number Twelve, you can rest. Get in the push-up position. Now, that is called the front leaning rest position. You can rest like that and contemplate your sins."

I can hear him walk away and yell at someone else. Can't sag, lock your elbows, think about something else. Front leaning rest—wonder what a back leaning rest position would be. The person who thought that up was undoubtedly a paratrooper. The gravel bites my palms; the pistol belt and canteen around my waist must weigh a ton. Damn! How long have I been here? One more minute and I'll lie down and take a drink. Pretty easy for those bastard cadre, always bragging that they run as much as we do. Big deal. They wear shorts and T-shirts and baseball caps; we wear fatigues and steel pots and pistol belts. So help me, if you don't come back in one minute I'll lie down.

The steel pot wins. I can't hold my head up. I try shifting my weight from arm to arm. My back sags. One more minute . . .

"Have you had enough rest, Number Twelve?" The voice comes from directly overhead; probably belongs to the owner of those two boots.

"Yes, Sergeant."

"Good. You can do ten push-ups."

My muscles scream, my body is on fire. ". . . one for Airborne." I lurch to my feet and stick out my left foot in time to catch myself.

"What direction are you facing, Number Twelve?"

"North, Sergeant." Why doesn't he stand still instead of weaving back and forth?

"Left face. Now do ten to the West . . . About face . . . Ten to the East . . . Right face . . . Don't forget the South—the south will rise again. Ten more."

My arm muscles almost refuse, and my back won't cooperate at all. I barely manage a whispered count. Back on my feet. Why don't things stand still? Why is the sky such a funny color?

"All right, Number Twelve, grab that line and get the trolley back to the tower."

I put the line over my shoulder and lean. My leg muscles have a mind of their own. Christ, I can't run a straight line. I can just make out the tower through the pink haze. It gets closer but the haze persists.

A voice reaches my ears from miles away. "Bring it in, Twelve." One last effort. The voice again: "Where have you been, Twelve? Get ten."

". . . Four . . ." I'm not going back to that mound ". . . Six" . . . Past the halfway point ". . . Nine" . . . They can take their "hit its" and "Airborne" and their jump school and shove it ". . . Ten" . . . Concentrate. No, you'll never make it. My body comes up in sections, like a snake's ". . . Airborne." Now you mothers, that's it. Ram it sideways. Damn, even the tower is moving.

"Take a place on the end of the bench, Twelve."

I almost forget to say "Clear, Sergeant." I collect my body into a runing stance, but the dust says my feet aren't clearing the ground. The black blur must be other men on the bench. I almost run into a T-shirt and baseball cap.

"Permission to speak, Sergeant."

"What is it, Twelve? And stand still."

Ah, you're not going to catch me. It's you moving and you only said that to get me mad. If only that pink haze would go away. "I need some water, Sergeant."

"If you have salt tablets, go ahead."

"Clear, Sergeant."

I fumble for the canteen and salt tablets. The warm water reopens my throat. More. Stomach spasms, settles. More. Pause. Sluice it around, get rid of the mucilage in the back. Another pull. There is no more. The haze starts to clear. I'm sweating again. Stare at the tower door. Can't take any more push-ups. The steel pot threatens to pull my head off.

A man in harness shuffles by the bench to the scorer's chair. "Roster Seventeen . . ."

"Feet apart, knees bent, elbows out, head up. Unsatisfactory jump, Seventeen. Make another."

"Fuck your stupid jump school and fuck you. I quit."

Everyone on the bench stiffens. Surely lightning will strike.

"Seventeen, you are an NCO in the United States Army. Such language will not be tolerated. Get ten for each time you swore and ten for being disrespectful."

His equipment flaps up and down as he does his squat jumps. He looks back at the scorer. "I said I quit."

"That will be ten for not saying the proper response when I gave you the order and ten for speaking without permission."

"I said I'm quitting."

"That will be ten more. You're still in the Army, Seventeen, and you will obey orders."

He barely makes it but his jaw is stubbornly clamped.

"You have on jump equipment, Seventeen. If you want to quit, you quit in the tower, where I ordered you to go originally.* You go up there and stand in the door and shout down to me that you quit." The scorer shouts to the tower, "Clear the door. We have a quitter coming up."

How do his knees manage to function after sixty squat jumps? The stairs must be agony. The jumpmaster is yelling and equipment rattles inside the box.

"Stand in the door."

The two-inch white numbers on Seventeen's helmet are clearly visible. His eyes flash hate.

"Roster number."

"I quit!" The words ring out over the entire area. The jaws clamp shut and . . . he jumps. The bottom of his boots aim right at the scorer. Two bounces and he rolls past on the cable toward the mound. Again he shuffles by the bench, his face twisted from fatigue and emotion. He stands defiantly in front of the scorer.

"Roster Seventeen, you failed to count. Unsatisfactory jump. Jump again."

"I told you I quit."

"The proper answer is 'Clear, Sergeant.' That will cost you ten. You said you quit, but you jumped. That will be ten for lying. Another ten for not running back from the mound. If you quit, you quit up there. If don't go up the tower you will be disobeying a lawful order. That could be very expensive for an NCO. Now get with it."

* If a man fails to jump the tower, his release slip is marked RTJT—Refused To Jump Tower, which precludes him from ever reapplying for airborne training and is also supposed to stigmatize the individual, proof that he is a "leg quitter," the lowest form of life. When a man quits, he can only obtain the slip the next day, so he reports to the school in the morning and while it is being made out (a procedure that coincidentally takes all day), the man is put on details working around the students, where he is constantly harassed and ridiculed as a "leg quitter."

He falls down once on the second series and twice on the third, but he finishes. He has to use his hands on the stairs to get up the tower.

More shouting, more rattling, and again, "Stand in the door . . . Roster number."

It comes out choked, but it comes out—"I quit." There is a split second in which it appears as if he will back out of the door. An anguished moan and he throws himself into the air. We can see his tears as he goes by.

Twice more the battle of wills takes place. Seventeen has found his own madness. Staggering when he comes by the bench, his arms and legs moving like a poorly stringed puppet's, he is operating on pure hatred.

A whistle blows. Quitting time.

"You didn't count, Seventeen. Unsatisfactory jump. Take off your harness and put it in the Conex container." The scorer finishes speaking, turns his back, and climbs down from his perch. Seventeen trembles uncontrollably.

In the formation I can feel my legs stiffening. Just a few more minutes to hang on.

The scorer walks down the line and stops in front of Seventeen. "Come back tomorrow, Seventeen. You'll make a good trooper. You won't quit." A sob wrenches from the student's chest. The cadreman steps back and yells, "Section Chiefs take over. Dismissed."

●   ●   ●

I put the last touches to my boots, stow them under the bed, and check the board-stiff fatigues for buttons and loose threads. The steel pot with its white *12* is ready —is it possible to hate a number? After methodically polishing the brass belt buckle back and front and running a pipe cleaner through the inside to make sure that there

is no residual polish, I wrap it carefully in a handkerchief.

I lie back on the bunk and think of tomorrow and
the routine. First the warning whistle and then the fall-in
signal. Two hundred and eighty men running like raped
apes to their formation positions, screaming like maniacs.
Whip the handkerchief off the belt buckle, take a fast
swipe at the boots. Inspection. It should be our turn tomorrow to be inspected in T-shirts—make sure it has no
holes. Be special emphasis on belt and boots. As usual
we'll be sweating before inspection is over. Then the run
—those starch-stiff fatigues will be sweat-dark to below
the crotch before that is over. Then the pull-up bar, wet
with sweat from the men who have gone before. The
PT pit—I squirm on the bed thinking about it—and our
wet bodies in that mixture of sand and sawdust, which
works its way under trousers and boots and sticks to
wet backs and chests. Five minutes after PT to get back
into shirts and helmets and in formation. Two hundred
and eighty men bending down, palms on the ground, legs
spread, while one man walks down the line with a hose,
spraying off the sand; then he walks down and washes
the front. So much for the spit-polished boots, starched
fatigues, and polished buckle.

Come right down to it, physically it's not that rough
—the run isn't too far and the PT isn't too long—but
that damned pit and putting on clothes over sand and
sawdust. And today at the tower, when I was sure I was
going to die—in another place, under different circumstances, it wouldn't have been easy but it wouldn't have
had such an overwhelming effect. Look how fast I dehydrated and how tight my chest became. It's that
damned unnecessary harassment that bludgeons the
mind. It's basic training again. No, it's more than that.

Here you can quit. It's your choice. Somehow it's worse because it is your choice. Had I known what it would be like would I have gone through with it? Ted's warning sounded like exaggeration. I sure went to a lot of trouble to put myself in this place—physicals, testing, all that crap to get a security clearance, dieting, running around the block every morning with people looking at me as if I were nuts.

Why do we do it? We could join sky-diving clubs if jumping from an airplane were all we wanted. For the young privates the jump pay is probably an incentive, but I've given up proficiency pay, separate ration allowance, and a good off-duty job to be here. After three weeks of this I will have earned the right to wear a set of silver wings on my chest—and who cares? Another paratrooper only notices if you're not wearing them, and nobody else knows what they mean, In Orientation they as much as admit that the main purpose of most of the harassment is so "you can prove you want to be a paratrooper more than anything else in the world." If all I had to look forward to was assignment to an Airborne division, I would have quit already. I guess I've always wanted to be a Jack McAllister and do something instead of just playing at it.

That must be it. How many times have I thought it and heard it from others on field exercises, "If this were only the real thing?" All that training and practice in Germany—and for what? So we could train and practice some more. NCOs and officers trying to instill seriousness and enthusiasm for what everyone knew to be games— playing at war—and all ranks secretly wishing something would *really* happen. How else, except in the real thing, can a soldier know if he has learned his lessons well? Special Forces training won't be easy, but it has a purpose; they are actually putting their training into practice. Wonder if I'll be as self-sufficient as those men I met in Germany? Probably not, but maybe I'll be good enough to make a team. Strange that an outfit requiring a high intelligence level and personal initiative makes you go through a jump school whose main purpose is to make you into a robot. Well, starting tomorrow, let your mind slip out of gear and quit fighting it.

THE METAL Capewell releases on the harness dig cruelly into my collar bones. I want to bend over and ease the weight of the chute from my shoulders. For three hours we've been waiting in line, on the aircraft. On my right, Brulet looks like he's going to cry. On my left, standing straight and easy, Vance is his normal cool self; he doesn't even appear to be sweating while the rest of us are soaked, and references to the 13 on his helmet bring only a small smile to his face.

The jumpmaster comes down our "stick" and breaks it between Brulet and me; those still left in the class between 1 and 11 fall in at the other end. I lead out, double timing after the jumpmaster toward a C-119—a Flying Boxcar. We halt short of the plane—funny, it's smaller than I had imagined. The jumpmaster checks out four jumpers lounging in the plane's shadow—one is an instructor, the other three are young officers who already have their wings—and they climb aboard.

The jumpmaster motions me forward, checks my harness and reserve, turns me around and passes the yellow nylon static line over my shoulder, and checks the back straps. I bend over, he taps me on the butt and tells me to get aboard. My heart pounds. Instead of getting on the tailgate as practiced in school we embark through the front door. The school instructor gives me a hand up and directs me to a rear seat next to one of the officers. As the plane fills up it becomes an oven filled with the sour smell of sweat. It's small and its decor is a maze of cables, wires, black boxes, and clamps. The officers look at us with tolerant amusement. I look at my surroundings with what I hope is an air of nonchalance.

The front door is locked and the jumpmaster calls for attention. "Flying time to the DZ * will be approximately twenty minutes. We will make three passes. First Sergeant Damon and the three officers will jump; you will remain seated until they jump. On the second pass half of each stick will jump; the second half will remain seated. If there is any trouble after takeoff and we are not at jump altitude, a bell will ring and you will lie sideways with your head to the front of the aircraft. If we are at jump altitude, I will signal you to hook up. There will be no time to check equipment. The second bell will be continuous and I will signal you to go. Everybody goes." (Some wag has already told us that without power the Boxcar has a glide path ratio of zero.)

Each motor in turn grinds, agonizingly turns over, and explodes into coughing life. The crew chief throws a fire extinguisher in the rear door and climbs aboard, locking the door behind him. At the end of the runway the motors are revved up, threatening to shake the plane to pieces. The heat is almost unbearable. The motors slowly rev up again and with a lurch we gain forward speed.

The motors' fluctuating drone makes me drowsy despite my excitement. It's finally going to happen. The months of red tape, the miles of running, the countless push-ups and squat jumps and harassment have all led

* Drop zone.

to this. The final PT test, which had me so worried, turned out to be easier than the daily PT. There had been no repeat of my bad day at the tower and I was never picked out again for personal harassment. Was I picked out that day or did my resentment make it seem that way? Is it possible that the harassment continued but I didn't notice it because my attitude changed?

Am I scared? No, I really don't think so. Will I remember to do everything right? That's pretty funny. Two nights ago, on my way to the shower, that wiseass yelled "hit it" and I remembered—the towel had gone one way, my shaving kit had scattered another and I was bent over at the two thousand count before I realized I'd been had. What did I tell Ted? "It won't take at my age." Ha!

The jumpmaster takes off the rear doors, letting in fresh air and raising the noise level. He walks up the plane and yells through cupped hands, "Is everybody going to jump?"

"Yes, Sergeant!" we roar back.

"What are you?"

"Airborne!"

"What?"

"Airborne!" The motor noise is drowned out.

He smiles, exuding a friendly paternalism instead of the usual sneering demeanor of the ground school cadre. His eyes move from man to man, making swift judgments. I do the same but can see only those across the aisle—Thirty-three still wears his helmet like it has no liner, and his hands are tightly clenched on top of the reserve. Forty-one appears to be praying. Thirty-seven, pale and having difficulty breathing, is trying to stare through the bottom of the plane. Thirty-eight meets my eyes, shifts them away. I can feel the excitement rising inside but I'm not nervous. Vance, beside me, smiles calmly. In three weeks as his roommate I've never heard him raise his voice or get angry or complain. Always cool and patient, with a quiet humor. The only time he indicated that the physical exertions were affecting him was when he commented, "I haven't had a hard-on since I started this business."

The crew chief says something to the jumpmaster, who faces us and holds up both hands with fingers outstretched. Ten minutes to go. Then the six-minute warning. The jumpmaster looks out the door, and the wind peels back the skin on his face, trying to force open his compressed mouth. The two men on each side who will jump first, stand, hook up, and check their gear. There is some conversation between the jumpmaster and one of the officers. One man steps into each door. The jumpmaster steps back, the green light comes on, the four men disappear. A safety NCO helps haul in the static lines and unhook them from the cable.

The plane banks, comes around for the next pass. The jumpmaster looks at us and then shows us the palm of his hand. "Get ready . . ." The words are lost in the noise of the motors. Foot in the aisle, hand on knee. His palm turns up, he raises his outstretched arm. "Stand up . . ." We rise and hook back the troop seats. I brace against the plane's roll. Hand out at shoulder level, he crooks his little finger and pumps his arm up and down. "Hook up . . ." I reach up and hook the snap on the cable and slip the small wire into the safety hole. My blood pounds in unison to the beat of the motors. Thumb and forefinger in an "okay." "Check static lines . . ." I make sure I'm holding the proper fold in the line next to the snap. Vance follows my line with his hand to make sure it flows over my shoulder to the chute on my back. The jumpmaster pats his chest. "Check equipment . . ." Vance goes over my back straps with one hand. I check the front. Hands cupped behind the ear. "Sound off for equipment check . . ." Feet stamping, voices yelling. Vance yells "Two okay," and slaps me on the butt. I stamp the floor and shout, "All okay." The safety NCO double-checks. The plane banks again, and levels off. The jump-master glances through the door, steps back, and stares into my eyes. Is he laughing? He flings his arm to the side and points. This time I can hear him: "Stand in the door . . ." I turn into the door, flinging the heavy snap to the end of the cable. Eyes straight ahead, palms flat against the outside of the aircraft, one toe over the edge, knees bent. The air blast tries to push me back.

I wait for the "go" poised ready to throw myself. Wait. I glance down. A small settlement passes by, cars move slowly along a road. Funny, I would have thought twelve hundred feet would look higher than this—I can see people walking. A large area of dark green pine trees is passing. Hell! There isn't any drop zone down there. The jumpmaster is playing games; the book says he's not supposed to have the first man in the door for more than ten seconds. I break the rules and turn my head to look at him. His face is only inches from my own, the skin crinkling around his eyes.

"How's it look, Twelve?"

"Great, Sergeant."

He grins. "Get ready then."

I turn back, the pushing blast now a friend cooling my sweaty body. I take a deep breath and draw in power from the glorious noise of the motors. I am conscious of the smooth coolness of the aluminum skin . . . I feel a rivet. Every nerve is alive. I want to shout to the world. My stomach has a top-of-a-new-ski-run feeling.

A winding river slices through a large patch of dark trees. A highway—Manchester Road? Sand, miniature men on the DZ. "Go!"

Push. "One thousand . . ." I can't hear it—I have thrown myself into the roar of ten Niagaras. A huge hand violently snaps me halfway around—a matchstick in a flash flood. "Two thousand . . ." I'm rolling slowly to my side. Why doesn't the ground seem to move? "Three thous . . ." A gentle tug. Abruptly Niagara is turned off. I'm suspended in a bubble. What beautiful silence. There is no world. I'm in heaven and I'll be here forever. I want to wrap myself in the balmy peace. It's been worth it.

Against my will my hands reach up for the risers, shattering my bubble. I look up and—son of a bitch! Wouldn't you know it would be me?

Two suspension lines are over my canopy, forming a Mae West.* I snap the risers, the lines move. Snap again, they're slipping. Again. The lines slip all the way over and the chute blossoms full. I look down and notice the ground coming up to meet me. Cadreman over there; better make a good PLF.† I'm falling very slowly. Feet together, knees slightly bent, hands on the risers, eyes on the horizon—relax. Down . . . over . . . up . . . running. The sand is soft, deep, and hot. I am ten feet tall and the whole world is beautiful.

"Roster Twelve. Was that you with the partial malfunction?" I hadn't heard the cadreman approach.

"Yes, Sergeant." I do my best to keep from my voice my pride in working it out.

"When you have a partial malfunction, Twelve, you

---

* Lines over the canopy (or an inversion) pinch the canopy in the center making two half canopies, giving the chute the appearance of an overlarge bra.
† Parachute Landing Fall.

are not supposed to play with it. That is why you have a reserve. Get ten."

"Clear, Sergeant." Back to earth.

●　　●　　●

I hobble up the ramp behind Vance. They sure have us loaded down—hanging below my reserve is my loaded combat pack and strapped to my side like a body splint is an M-1 rifle. Our third jump of the day, this will be our fifth and last for the course. Tomorrow will be a day off; the next day are graduation ceremonies. It has been a long haul but this is the end.

We flop in the seats and fasten seat belts. Half a dozen straphangers,* including a chaplain, climb up the ramp and take the seats nearest the door.

The jumpmaster signals ten minutes and walks down the aisle. When he approaches us, Vance motions and the sergeant bends down.

"I'm not going to jump, Sergeant," Vance speaks calmly. I look at him in disbelief.

"What?" The jumpmaster shares my shock.

Vance repeats the statement in the same dispassionate voice and looks levelly at the jumpmaster.

"You can't quit now, Thirteen. This is the last jump, just the one and you graduate. Think of all the work you've done and what you have gone through to come this far. You don't want it all to go for nothing, do you?" The jumpmaster sounds almost human, pleading and coaxing.

"That's exactly what I don't want, Sergeant."

* People, usually from another unit, trying to make a pay jump because for one reason or another they haven't jumped for three months.

The jumpmaster, completely baffled, straightens up, walks to the end of the plane, and returns with the chaplain.

The chaplain starts to put his hand on Vance's shoulder, hesitates, pulls it back. "Son, I know how you feel. We all feel that way at times. But you have jumped four times and you know it is safe. I'll go with you if that will help. It is no disgrace to be afraid to jump. It's by overcoming our fear that we become men. Now, how about it?"

Vance answers, self-assured. "I don't think you do understand, Chaplain. I didn't say I was afraid. I said I wasn't going to jump. I've never been afraid to jump. I believe that anybody—anybody—who jumps from an aircraft knowing he is afraid is an insane idiot."

Both the jumpmaster and the chaplain stiffen visibly.

"If you aren't afraid, why don't you jump? Why quit now?" The chaplain's voice has taken on an edge.

"I'm not quitting, Chaplain," Vance explains patiently. "I'm not going to jump. Look—if I make this jump, I automatically graduate, right?" Two heads nod. "And if I don't jump, that means I can never again be assigned to an Airborne unit. If I jump, I automatically become a paratrooper. And that, sir, is nothing, and I won't jump for nothing."

The jumpmaster's face reflects puzzlement, the chaplain turns red.

"What does that mean, Thirteen?" the jumpmaster asks.

"It means, Sergeant, that of all the things I don't want to be, paratrooper heads the list. I don't want your Airborne wings or your Airborne mentality. For three weeks you have harassed us, run us, and debased us to make us into what you want us to be—paratroopers. I can't let that happen to me without losing my self-respect. I would rather have that than the wings."

The jumpmaster's face mingles anger, scorn, confusion, and hate. He keeps opening his mouth and closing his fists. He can't find the words. Finally he screams, "Get to the front of the aircraft!"

The stick is moving out the door. I glance back at Vance; our eyes meet. Come on. There's still time. He knows but shakes his head. I'm angry. I've been betrayed. He has taken the joy out of it. The sense of accomplishment is gone. I close my mind to his words.

"One thousand . . . Two thousand . . ."

A CLASSROOM in a yellow frame building: gray steel desks in rows, two chairs behind each. I choose the right aisle and stop at a window desk with an empty chair.

"This place taken?" I ask the sergeant sitting next to the window.

He motions me in, then half stands with an outstretched hand. "My name is Jon Martensen," he says in what sounds like a German accent.

I give him my hand and name, slightly amused by the formality of the introduction. Taller than I by a couple of inches, he gives the impression of tough leanness. His sparse blond hair is cropped extremely short. I glance at the jump wings sewn on his fatigues—the star and wreath of a master jumper. He cuts his hair by choice, not because he is a recent jump school graduate. His face, dominated by a large, almost beaked nose, has a Slavic look. The five fading stripes on his arm indicate he has been a sergeant first class for some time.

There seems to be an abundance of six-stripers in the barracks-turned-classroom; the remainder are SFCs. Judging by age, many of them must have from fifteen to seventeen years of service, and I wonder why they have volunteered for this training. I recognize only Master

Sergeant Reed at the desk behind me and Brulet across the aisle.

I wonder if, like Reed, all these senior NCOs have worked for years in Infantry Operations and Intelligence. I hope I did the right thing by letting personnel talk me out of the medical training in favor of Operations and Intelligence, for if they assume that we all have years of experience in the infantry, I could be in trouble.

Ten NCOs led by a captain, all dressed in short-sleeved khakis, file in. The officer, old for a captain, introduces himself as Le Boeuf and gives a brief welcome to the O and I committee, introducing the NCOs. He testifies to their expertise and experience. His seamed face and slouched body inside the ill-fitting uniform look comic alongside the tall NCOs in their severely tailored uniforms. Most are master sergeants; all appear self-assured and confident.

I recognize some of the names from conversations with Ted. Master Sergeant Phelps—one of those who look completely at ease while standing at attention in an impeccable uniform—is a live recruiting poster; his weight-lifter biceps completely fill the short sleeves of his shirt. Lacey, at least six feet three inches tall, is incredibly skinny but in his hollow, cadaverous face his eyes glow with perpetual excitement and mischief—a fun instructor and a genius, Ted says. And then Latham, with a paternal smile, looking more like a colonel than a colonel; the word is that he is a perfectionist who will kill you with written homework assignments.

The remainder of the hour is spent making up a seating plan, passing out training schedules, signing for manuals, and selecting a class leader. The latter is accomplished by the six-stripers comparing time in grade as master sergeants. White, an overweight combat veteran from the 101st Airborne, wins; Reed is the alternate.

Instruction begins. In less than five days Sergeant Phelps takes us through the Map Reading Manual, takes us on a land navigation course, and examines us. His instruction technique is as flawless as a well-rehearsed movie, and high exam grades testify to his effectiveness.

The school routine is like a vacation after the recent physical exertion, and the informality between students and instructors is amazing. Smoking in class is permitted and there is a coffee break each morning and afternoon. A real vacation.

To the students the instructors are repositories of secrets and mystery, men who have taken part in strange missions in strange places. They don't talk about these things, but the impression is given by an apparently slipped word, a raised eyebrow, a knowing wink, a benign smile that they possess great secrets. They continually emphasize that they are not spooks * but in such a way as to heighten the suspicion that such activities are at least common diversions. Rumors and speculation about the instructors' missions fly. Direct questions are answered with a smile and an admonition that such things should not be talked about. Being photographed, except for ID purposes, is avoided. Will we ever gain the knowledge and expertise of these assured NCOs and be selected for missions and be privy to such information?

Any illusions about this being a vacation are dispelled by the start of the third week. It is a rare night that isn't spent doing eight hours of written homework, and spare moments are spent catching up with the required-reading list. I wish it were over but I am enjoying it.

It's a good class—lots of participation in the classroom and free exchange of information out of it. During

* Spy, cloak-and-dagger specialist, agent.

bull sessions the class breaks into self-selected groups that are not cliques. My group includes Martensen, Reed, and Brulet. The only explanation for our grouping seems to be that we have the highest grades, although Brulet is the only one regarding it a competition. Except for White and Harrison everyone's grades are high, and it is now obvious that most of the students held responsible jobs in their old outfits. Only a few have not had some college training.

As I originally suspected, Reed used to play football, but his bull neck and scarred face are misleading. He's not all "gung-ho" muscle and wind; he's a damned good student and must have been a good top kick before joining Special Forces. Brulet, as I suspected, is a make-out artist who spends good time working angles and politicking, trying to butter up the instructors. He makes no bones about it and refuses to be insulted, and his almost professional talent for dialect jokes and satire makes him bearable. Martensen is the class "brain," but most think him standoffish, perhaps because of his accent and his habit of looking down his nose, which gives him an arrogant air. His seriousness possibly scares away many people; he has already read most of the books on the recommended-reading list. He and I share a room now. His knowledge of communism is prodigious, his loathing of it contagious.

MARTENSEN IS AMAZING. In addition to his studies, he is also completing the Series Ten—pre-commission correspondence course—from Fort Benning. He works like a man possessed and at times his dedication is a little frightening, but he is a good roommate. He has even talked me into running once a day to keep in shape —a good thing, because I am tempted to be lazy now.

During the week our spare time is spent making up problems in tactics and intelligence, picking each other's brains every spare moment. Saturday morning is spent in the library, the afternoon at studying in the laundromat, the evening in catching up and getting ahead.

Sunday. Leisure time by the pool at the main NCO club; by mutual agreement studies are not discussed.

I heave from the pool and move to a deck chair leaving a wet trail of dark prints on the light cement. Drying my face with a towel, I grope for a cigarette—it tastes of chlorine. Damn, but this is great—sure beats that hot barracks. This is the best time, early, before the church crowd and the Saturday revelers arrive with their children and their hangovers. I stretch and relax, watching Martensen, determined, methodical, stroke off one more length of the pool. He attacks the water grimly— swimming is just necessary exercise, not pleasure or recreation. I wonder if he enjoys anything at all. He finally finishes and takes the chair beside me.

We talked lazily, and as usual got around to his favorite subject—his Baltic homeland.

"I have a mission to help my people—to free my country and throw out the Russians. When I was a boy, the Russian Communists stole the country, or really, it was given to them while the world did nothing. Chamberlain was criticized for Munich, but Roosevelt was no better about my country—and that was long before Munich."

He went on to tell me of the destruction of his family and how he had been sent to a refugee camp until the arrival of the Americans. After that he played the black market, educated himself, and finally arrived in the States. He joined the Army and became a citizen.

"One day I will go back to my country. In the meantime I prepare myself. I joined the 11th Airborne and went with them to Germany in fifty-five as part of my preparation. I must try to become a perfect soldier. At the Seventh Army NCO Academy, I learned the value of discipline and even taught there. I worked with the Long Range Reconnaissance Patrols. That is when I first met the Special Forces.

"When I found they were making detailed area studies of Russian-occupied countries for the purpose of jumping in to wage guerrilla warfare, I knew I must join them. I could not join immediately so everything up to now has been preparation. I thought for sure they would go into Hungary in fifty-six, but I guess the politicians stopped them. Maybe it is like they tell us in training—the American people are not yet mentally capable of guerrilla warfare because it is dirty and cruel. They must be worked up to it a little at a time and then they'll have the guts for fighting. Someday soon they'll be ready, and when it comes I will be prepared.

"I already speak German and soon I will speak Russian. I have relearned my language. The Communists were not satisfied with taking our riches and displacing our people; they even changed the language. Now, I will learn all there is to know about guerrilla warfare and go back to Europe. When the balloon goes up I want to be on the first plane, leading the first stick of the first 'A' team into the Baltic. The Communists will die."

The only time his true feelings show through Martensen's normally iron control is when he talks about communism. He's really not talking to me—it's like he is reciting a prayer. His nostrils pinch, his blazing eyes focus far beyond the pool, the backs of his clenched hands are white. I hope I am on that same plane.

"What about Asia and South America, Jon? As far as guerrilla warfare is concerned that seems to be where the action is. Instead of going to Europe, it seems you could learn more there."

He snorts disdainfully and looks along his nose. "Only the principles are adaptable to my country. The techniques are not. I cannot waste my time and talents in such a place as Viet-Nam. I would not blend; there are no blue-eyed, blond-haired gooks."

FOR THE PAST FEW DAYS you have been learning the principles and techniques of psychological interrogation. You know that with time a subject will give you the information you desire. It is the recommended way to get information from a suspect or prisoner, and the only way to get reliable information—the subject volunteers it." Sergeant Lacey's lank body drapes over a corner of the table.

"Today we will learn about countermeasures to hostile interrogation—how you as the subject can resist interrogation techniques. Sergeant Masterson is passing out copies of a translation from the NKVD * interrogation manual; this is another type of interrogation."

The casual, almost jovial, language used to describe the details of the "Airplane Ride," the Cold-Hot Water Treatment, the lowering of a man's testicles into a jeweler's vise heighten the audience's involuntary shivers.

"As it says, these are tried and true methods, guaranteed to bring on a severe case of oral diarrhea. Few men

* Narodni Kommisariat Vnutrennikh Del—People's Commissariat for Internal Affairs (Security Police)—originally known as the *Cheka* (*Chrezvychainaya Komissya*), later as the OGPU (Ob'yedinennoye Gosudarstvennoye Politicheskoye Upravlenie, and more recently as the MVD.

can persevere against such methods for any significant period of time. Except for fanatics—like religious zealots in a holy war—even those who have nothing to say will invent something with this added motivation. This is why, time permitting, the psychological methods are more reliable.

"If you are operating a guerrilla net in a foreign country, you must not be taken prisoner, because in your special position you will have knowledge beyond a normal guerrilla's and are sure to get special attention if captured. You will be interrogated by experts. I have no intention of becoming a prisoner—I'm under no illusions as to how long I would last with a pair of pliers wrapped around my testicles. I recommend that those of you who are Catholics and have scruples about taking a pill try to make a break and get yourself shot. If an interrogator suspects his subject has any information, that old 'Name, Rank, Serial Number, and Date of Birth' routine will mean nothing. If an operation depends on certain information, the rights of one man must be ignored."

Lacey's voice keys high, describing variations of the methods on the paper. His eyes are animated and he is obviously enjoying the effect of his words on the class. His vivid and detailed descriptions raise two questions in his listeners' minds: How long could I endure such treatment? Could I perform these horrors on another human? A third question occurs to me: Can I learn to hate deeply enough to do either?

"By now it should be obvious that it is impossible to withhold info from an expert interrogator. For us, that is dangerous knowledge, because there is the temptation to say, 'If I am going to talk eventually, why not do it before I suffer pain and mutilation or my mind is reduced to a cabbage?' Remember that once the interrogator has you talking, there will be the problem of convincing him that you have no more to tell; once convinced, he will have no further use for you except perhaps for propaganda purposes. Once the commies grab you, it is only a matter of time before they kill you.

"If you are captured, it is imperative that you not divulge any accurate information for at least twenty-four hours, by which time the base camp should know you are a prisoner and will take appropriate action to displace the camp. Don't count on being rescued; rarely will the benefits of your release outweigh the losses necessary to effect it.

"We have discussed the futility of trying to outsmart an interrogator by lying, since it will be only a matter of time before he finds the truth and uses the lie against you. There is also the chance that by fabricating a story, you will accidentally hit upon a truth unknown to you. One suggested course of action is to anticipate capture and, before launching a mission, carefully rehearse a plausible story that the enemy will need at least twenty-four hours to check. Your story must not be easily told— the longer it takes to tell, the more plausible it will seem. Your failure to return, to make radio contact or send some other signal, will alert base camp that something is wrong and give them sufficient time to move or go into hiding. Once the lie is discovered and the truth forced from you, the information will be of no benefit to the enemy.

"Or the base camp can displace as soon as you have left on the mission so that you don't know where it is. This is why if a guerrilla net is compartmented, the capture of one man can compromise the whole net. The . . . Yes, Sergeant Harrison?"

"Sergeant Lacey, the name of this class is 'Countermeasures to Hostile Interrogation,' but you have spent most of the period telling us there are no countermeasures. If this is true, then the only reason for teaching them, it seems to me, is so that we'll know how to use them. Are you suggesting we use these methods?"

The class laughs, and Lacey looks down at the floor, creating a dramatic pause. When he raises his head, his face is solemn but his deep-set eyes are dancing. "We can't tell you that, Sergeant Harrison. The Mothers of America wouldn't approve." The class bursts into laughter at the sarcastic cynicism. "Furthermore," a conspiratorial wink, "we will deny that any such thing is taught or intended.

"When you are in a foreign country as part of a guerrilla organization, you will not be doing the interrogating. Your job is to teach the various methods of interrogation to your indigenous counterpart. It would be very bad form for you, as an outsider, to do the questioning—especially if it gets nasty. The forces opposing your guerrillas will probably be a native, be the same color, have the same religion. If you display a willingness to harm the natives, even though they are the enemy, it could be misunderstood by your guerrillas as prejudice. The indigenous guerrilla leader must believe that the idea for a course of action comes from himself; your control must be by suggestion. If the indigenous fighters learn that they are doing the bidding of an outside power, you may have a very short tour.

"You know that information gained through force or torture is not likely to be reliable. But keep in mind that psychological methods are time-consuming and require a great degree of sophistication on the interrogator's part and proper facilities in which to be conducted. Every guerrilla cannot be trained as an interrogation specialist, and in many countries it will take time to prove that psychological methods are not a pure waste of time.

"Ideally, prisoners will be brought to the trained interrogator for questioning, but this won't always be practical. For instance, assume that a guerrilla unit on a mission is approaching the target area. The unit has taken a prisoner who, it is believed, can furnish information on guard positions, booby traps, mines, and other dispositions. The lives of many of the guerrillas and, more important, the success of the mission, may depend on it. Even if a trained interrogator is on hand, if the prisoner is not disposed to talk voluntarily, it is hardly the time or place to be concerned with the Geneva Conventions.

"It should also be pointed out that prisoners present problems. While enemy prisoners are essential as an information source, rarely will any one prisoner have much of usable information. Before a prisoner is taken, his value as an informant should be weighed against the liabilities of having him on hand.

"Mobility is a guerrilla's best protection. He must be able to move on a moment's notice—fast. Land is something over which to maneuver, not to be held, not to be defended. Only in the last steps of the insurgent movement, when the guerrillas are ready to phase into conventional units, can holding land be considered.

"Prisoners have an adverse effect on mobility. Obviously, prisoner-of-war camps cannot be established if the ability to move quickly is to be maintained. Feeding prisoners strains supplies, and guerrillas cannot afford to have to establish complex supply lines which large numbers of men will have to defend; nor can significant numbers of men be utilized as guards. These things are especially true in the earlier stages of an insurgent movement.

"This means, of course, that you have a disposal problem. Prisoners who have not learned too much about the guerrillas or their net can be turned back to their own as propaganda weapons to testify to their good treatment. At times, in fact, it is a good tactic to take prisoners solely for this purpose, but it must be remembered that in all probability they will fight against the guerrillas. Of course, any prisoner who has penetrated the net cannot be allowed to return and compromise it. It is conceivable that some prisoners can be converted to the guerrilla cause. For those who won't cooperate, there has to be a more permanent means of disposal— again, this must be done by the indigenous leader.

"Killing prisoners may sometimes be essential for survival but it raises another problem: if the enemy forces learn that prisoners are being executed, it may initially cause fear in the ranks but it will lead to increased future resistance to avoid capture. This will cut down enemy desertions and lose sympathy for the guerrilla cause. Thus, there is a time to take prisoners and a time to dispose of them—and the opposite is just as true . . .

"As you know, this class is classified and you are cautioned not to discuss any of the material covered. Let me emphasize: *you* have not been told to kill or torture prisoners. If you have qualms or a weak stomach, you don't have the proper mental attitude and are psychologically unsuited for what must be done; in which case, I recommend that you get out before you endanger those who know what must be done. That's classified also, and I'll deny I ever said it. Thank you, gentlemen. That's all for today."

STOP THEM! Don't let them pull back!" The blond, big-boned lieutenant's words are lost in the explosion of a mortar round. The dozen or so Vietnamese and the three Americans press harder against the earth dike, dirt clods and shrapnel whistle overhead, invisible machine-gun bullets try to eat away the bank.

The lieutenant again shouts at the swarthy Vietnamese commander: "Make them get down! They'll all be killed trying to get over those paddy dikes. The planes will be here soon. Make them stop!" Again his words are lost, this time in the sharp cracks from the rifles of the two American NCOs. Their efforts draw the attention of the enemy machine gun and they pull in their heads.

The younger NCO shouts to his partner, "See if you can get to that BAR and give the gunner a kick in the ass." The sergeant slithers down the line behind the barricade, hesitating for only a moment as the shower of dirt from another mortar round rains around him. The Vietnamese gunner has a bloody sleeve and his leg is sticking out at an unnatural angle; he moans softly, hopelessly. The American starts the BAR chattering, sending death toward the distant treeline.

Other men huddle behind each dike of the dry paddies, to escape the waves of searching bullets. A man

turns, breaks, runs—and is cut down on his third step.
The world is the inside of a boiler being worked on by a
hundred riveters. Two mortars explode almost simultaneously and five men get up and start running back—one
makes it to the next dike, the others are sent sprawling
and screaming into the black earth. A half dozen still
forms mark the forward advance of the three columns
before the wall of fire was laid down from the treeline.
Exploding mortars force more men to attempt a break;
they are searched out by the rifle and machine-gun fire.
Only a few shoot back and even fewer are aiming.

Suddenly the lieutenant starts to pound the shoulder
of the Vietnamese at his side. "They're here! They're
here!" He points to six armed helicopters as they peel off
and start a run at the treeline from the flank. The gunfire
covers the sound of their approach. The enemy has seen
them and the fire from across the paddies slackens.

White smoke threads from the lead chopper into the
trees and the houses they hide. Orange flashes spring up
and sounds of exploding rockets float across to the men
in the paddies. The other choppers follow their leader,
unloading as they come. As the fifth starts his rockets
streaking on their way, the leader completes his turn,
ready to start a second run.

Bullets again race across the open area, this time
toward the trees from which a great gray and black cloud
is rising.

"Move up! Move up! *Di ra! Tien len!*"

English and Vietnamese commands mingle with a
bugle call, and a ragged line of screaming men are half
running toward the trees, shooting wildly. The choppers,
rockets unloaded and machine guns empty, turn toward
home.

Running, stumbling, reloading, shooting, the tiger-suited line swarms into the treeline. Bullets whine off brush, cutting branches cleanly, and swarm like hornets past the smoking ruins of the houses. Spurts of dust trace a path of dancing bullets from a carbine frozen on automatic. The sound of gunfire diminishes and is replaced by the soldiers' throaty shouting. The Vietnamese commander, his executive officer, and two platoon leaders assemble in the shell-pocked center of the village. The three Americans move to join them.

Thatched roofs burn on most of the houses. Those with reed and wood walls are almost burned to the ground; those with mud-clay are gutted with whole walls missing. The area is an inferno. Broken trees lean with drooping arms, flakes of ash settle on the bodies of live victors and dead victims. Torn and broken bodies litter the area, their clothes blown off by the rocket explosions. A brown leg with a dirty foot lies beside a well, and two children clasped in a permanent embrace are the concern of only a cloud of flies. The vacant-eyed man cuddling his intestines can't see the Bata boot that topples him from his Buddha position, and a naked baby paws at its dead mother's breasts.

From a smoldering ruin two soldiers carry a skinny girl of eight or nine, a hand under each arm to keep her frantically flailing feet off the ground; her child voice screams in fear and anger, her matchstick arms try to wrench free. Streaks in her grimy face trace the path of her tears. Head jerking from side to side, her dark eyes widen, almost filling her tiny face, as she takes in the horror of the remains of her village. Her struggles and screaming stop abruptly. She twists free and scurries on her stem legs, miniature black pajamas flapping, toward her baby brother and dead mother. She picks the protesting child from the dirt and blood, and clutches it to her small frame. Ignoring the soldiers, she walks a short distance and sits down, rocking her little brother and crooning a squeaky song.

Soldiers ransack the houses that aren't burning, collecting trophies of little value, chattering and yelling like excited children. Women, children, and old men dragged from the houses are herded into the center of the village, and as each house yields its last souvenir it is put to the torch. An occasional explosion announces a grenade flushing out a hole or expediting the destruction inside a house. An old man dressed in pajama bottoms is dragged forward. An old crone claws at a soldier, a torrent of words pouring from her pink-stained lips. She is thrown aside but gets up to try again. A burst from a carbine sits her abruptly into the dust, and she stares stupidly at the blood on the front of her dirty white blouse. Another woman starts to run back into her burning house, and a soldier clubs her with the stock of his carbine; there is a sickening crunch and he kicks her in rage when he finds the wood is broken.

Finally, there is only the crackling of flames and the babbling of soldiers who stand behind the villagers, their rifles at the ready.

The lieutenant wipes his flushed face with his camouflage hat and turns to the younger sergeant. "How many casualties do we have, Sergeant?"

"The interpreter says seven dead and sixteen wounded. One of the wounded probably won't make it but most of them aren't in bad shape."

"Not as bad as I thought. We've found at least thirty-seven VC bodies—no telling how many they dragged away. Both you men okay? . . . Good." He slaps them on the shoulder and his teeth gleam whitely in the darkened face.

There is a commotion behind the assembled villagers, who give way as four soldiers drag a young man in black shorts by his feet into the center. His arms are tied behind his back at the biceps and the wrists, the commo wire digging cruelly into the flesh. One shoulder is raw as a result of the dragging, and one leg has been broken below the knee by a bullet.

The company commander bends over him, brandishing his .45 automatic and barking questions. The youth is silent. The commander straightens up, snaps orders to the soldiers, and backs away. Two soldiers hold the prisoner's head while the others take turns pouring water fetched from the well into his nose and mouth. The older of the two American NCOs starts forward but is restrained by his partner.

"Goddamn it. They'll drown him."

"Don't interfere. It's their show."

"But he's a prisoner."

The lieutenant snaps around and looks at the NCO as if he has lost his senses. "That is enough, Sergeant. Shut up."

One of the soldiers, irritated by the prisoner's continued stubbornness, gives the broken leg one kick, another. The shattered bone shows through tortured flesh. The prisoner—his face twisted and distorted with pain, streaming with tears—still refuses to talk. He keeps his mouth closed except when forced to open it to pour in more water.

The natty Vietnamese executive officer, his trim mustache quivering in agitation, shouts at the soldiers and. they stand back from the prisoner. The impassive villagers move closer together and exchange glances—

something in the officer's tone or gesture. The little exec whips a knife from his belt and kneels beside the man, grabbing a handful of hair and yanking up his head. He twists until the youth's face is turned to his tormentor and then passes the blade back and forth before the pain-filled eyes. The blade traces a thin line down the bony chest to a point just above the navel. The knife is pressed deep against the bare gut while a question is screeched. Blood around the young man's mouth indicates that he has bitten his tongue or through his lip. The question is screeched again—silence. The mustached exec is livid with anger. Again he shouts at the prisoner . . . slowly his weight shifts to his knife arm . . . the blade disappears into the man as if he were soft butter.

A piercing wail of pure agony rips the hot smoky air as the blade continues into the ground. The officer jerks the knife out and walks away in disgust. The prisoner lies still and only the convulsive movement of his chest shows he is still alive.

The senior American NCO turns away . . .

"My God. What's *he* doing?"

Mon, the tall Vietnamese platoon leader, straddles the dying youth's thighs and drives a large knife into the bloody gut, extending the opening in one upward slash. The prisoner rises off the ground, rigid and arched from the waist, face distorted, eyes bulging, screaming like all the horrors of hell. Mon's face flashes annoyance and he slams a backhanded fist into the unhuman face, knocking the body flat, and continues his butchering. The body gives a few jerks, quivers, is still. Mon shoves his hand into the stinking hole and brings out the gall bladder. Grinning triumphantly, he holds his gory trophy overhead for all to see.

The sergeant, frozen with shock since his last exclamation, manages to find words again as the blood returns to his face. "This has got to be reported . . . it's horrible. Those men should be jailed." The words tumble over each other.

"Damn it, Dick, calm down before they hear you. This is your first time out—it's always a shock the first time, I suppose, but you get used to it. Relax."

"Relax? Get used to it? What are you—animals?" He is almost shouting.

"Sergeant," the lieutenant breaks in tersely, "I told you to shut up. And you'd better start smiling; they're starting to look at us."

"You mean you're not going to report this atrocity?"

"Jesus Christ, Dick, what's wrong with you? We didn't do it—they did. We're not animals, but you have to be practical."

"What's practical about killing a prisoner? That's no way to get information. It makes no sense. I don't think they expected or wanted information."

"Sergeant, there's an old saying: 'If you can't stand the heat, get out of the kitchen.' I just don't understand your attitude. If this game is too rough for your sensitivities, apply for an office job. Get this straight: the man they killed was a Viet Cong—a communist—and we're here to kill commies. Thirty minutes ago those men were terrified. They thought they were going to die. If those choppers had arrived five minutes later, most of them would have panicked and been killed and we would have been all alone. That kind of fear isn't nice. Now look at them. They're less scared; they feel brave. The dead man is proof of their power, and the platoon leader will wear that piece of gut around his neck as an amulet—a permanent reminder that they are men and that they have luck."

"Sure, Lieutenant, but what do you suppose they think?" He gestures to the villagers. "Women and children watching. What do they think? Look at them; they hate us."

"So a few women and children get killed and a prisoner died under interrogation—tough shit. Teach 'em a damned good lesson. They're all VC or at least helping them—same difference. You can't convert them, only kill them. Don't lose any sleep over those dead children—they grow up to be commies too. I'll admit a bullet would have been nicer, but we don't interfere. We're three men and there's a hundred of them. They already resent our presence; we endanger them, but we're tolerated because we can bring in air strikes when they get in a jam and because we pay them. We could disappear out here, so don't rock the boat. A report would only alienate the platoon leader, and he's one of our best men, one of the few the men will follow; we can't afford to lose him. This is a war and we have to stop the commies any way we can, using whatever we've got. Besides," the lieutenant continues, throwing his arm around the NCO's shoulder, "if you make an official report, it will cause a lot of embarrassment for Special Forces and MACV. They know what's going on and they may not like it, but they have to be practical too—it's an old story. Hell, man, cheer up; this is a big victory—enjoy it. We have a kill ratio of five to one!"

●　●　●

The murder described actually happened. I have refrained from giving detailed descriptions of the principals and locale, because it would serve no purpose nor add anything to the point of the story to indict or embarrass individuals. Any one of a half dozen similar incidents could illustrate the point as well: these are not "bad" men—they could be sitting in your living room tonight; Mon's knife is in mine.

REEADY FOR THE FINAL examination this afternoon, Brulet?" Reed takes a tentative sip of steaming coffee.

"Not as ready as I'd like to be. I just don't seem to have the time for studying. Pass the sugar, Dunc."

"If you had spent less time socializing at the club and running off to the headquarters crying about getting a PCS for your family, you would have had time," Reed shoots back.

Brulet shrugs. "You call it socializing, I call it good business. I want to have a good job waiting for me when this is over. You may not approve, but I have an assignment to the Fifth and I got the PCS, so you can't hurt my feelings." He grins and adds, "Eat your heart out."

"Sure, and those guys who had a real hardship and more talent had to quit because they didn't have your gift of gab. If you had the hardship you claim, you couldn't spend all that time in the club. How about you, Dunc—ready for this afternoon?"

"I don't feel ready, which is probably a good sign. Thank God for these four hours of review. I had almost forgotten some of this stuff was on the schedule. How about you?"

Reed laughs, "Oh, I'll pass but I don't think I'll set

the world on fire. Martensen here is probably the only one not worried. Actually the four of us have no sweat; we already have our seven hundred points. Right, Martensen?"

"No, I am not worried. I take the examination to see how much I have learned. The points mean nothing; seventy percent for this work is too low. If it had not been for fingerprinting and photography, people like White and Harrison would not be here. They should not be here—they are stupid. Men who make only seventy percent in map reading should not be NCOs. The course is good, but the scoring system is bad. All that score proves is that three out of ten times they use a map they will be wrong. Someday those men will have 'A' teams * and they will get people killed."

I glance quickly around the almost empty coffee shop to see if anyone has overheard Martensen—such speeches do not endear him to his classmates.

"I think everyone agrees that it was a good course," Brulet says. "In fact, it's some of the best instruction I've ever seen . . ."

Reed agrees. "Beats the NCO Academy. In fact, the only comparable classroom instructors I've seen were the ones I had in helicopter school."

"Helicopter school?" I ask. "You never told us that. How come you never graduated?"

"Stubbornness, I guess. Oh, I learned to fly—I even have a commercial license—but I just couldn't fly by their book. I went through all the pre-flight training, and

---

* Units of 2 officers and 10 enlisted men, all specialists in communications, medicine, intelligence, weapons, fortifications, and demolition. By early 1967, according to *The New York Times*, they had established between seventy-five and a hundred outposts in hostile territory.

before they finally turned me loose, I could fly as well as some of the instructors, and a damned sight better than most they graduate. But something kept me from doing turns and approaches for landings their way—I like mine better—so they washed me out on the basis that I had suicidal tendencies."

"From the things you told me you did in the war and other escapades, they may be right," Brulet comments.

Reed laughs. "There's no fun in always being careful like you. When we get 'A' teams, your cautiousness and working the angles isn't going to help when the chips are down. Watch me when I get mine, Brulet. It's going to be the best-trained, toughest, guttiest team in Special Forces, and there'll be no room for a man who won't take chances and play the margin."

"Well, before I hear a war story, I think I'll use the rest of the lunch hour going over my notes for the test." I pick up my empty cup and stand.

"I'll go with you," Martensen says. The other two give us a languid wave.

●   ●   ●

The only sound in the classroom is the hum of the fans in their losing battle against the heat. I take my fat notebook to another table so Martensen and I won't disturb each other.

I start skimming. Strange reference material for a U.S. Army school—Mao, Che, Tito, Ho, Stalin. Someone had commented that the first principle of guerrilla warfare should be to learn from winners.

●   ●   ●

Special Forces formed 1952 (what a shock that was; I had never heard of them until 1956 in Germany) . . . to organize, train, direct, and equip indigenous peoples of foreign countries in guerrilla warfare, to harass and overthrow unpopular governments hostile to the United States . . . When Russians attack across Europe, teams will be dropped into predetermined Eastern European countries to organize the oppressed peoples against their communist masters . . . cut supply lines . . . guerrillas no substitute for regulars . . . effective only when coordinated with regulars . . . Historical references: Russian partisans and Red Army against the Nazi invasion forces.

Organization of guerrilla units . . . cells . . . clandestine communications . . . winning the people's hearts and minds . . . psychological warfare . . . no insurgent movement can sustain itself without the popular support of the people . . . propaganda . . . the people are to the guerrilla as the water is to the fish . . . assassination teams . . . sabotage squads . . . agents . . . selective terrorism . . . guerrilla discipline . . . warning nets . . . political direction of insurgency. *Mao.*

Flexibility . . . adaptability of basic principles to particular area . . . patience . . . necessity of rest . . . living in terrain not considered inhabitable . . . the hammock. *Che.*

Don't interfere with internal politics . . . advise but don't lead . . . don't offend nationalism . . . escape plans . . . internal security. *Tito.*

Steps of insurgency . . . civic action . . . the enemy as supply depot . . . morale . . . phasing guerrillas into conventional forces . . . soldiers must help the peasants . . . political indoctrination. *Ho.*

Methods of infiltration . . . initial contacts . . . recruiting not difficult in areas under communist domination . . . cannot invent dissatisfaction, must already be seeds and a cause . . . safe houses . . . counterparts . . . the "A" team is eventually the nucleus of a regiment-sized headquarters . . . you are too valuable to be killed; after leadership is developed, stay away from battles . . . control guerrillas by controlling supplies and communications . . . training management . . . cadre . . . intelligence nets . . . five-paragraph operation orders . . . analysis of courses of enemy action . . . terrain compartments . . . corridors . . . avenues of approach . . . fields of fire . . . coastal hydrography . . . records . . . enemy order of battle . . . fingerprint identification . . . binoculars as telephoto lenses . . . "one-time" crypto pads . . . sources of information . . . truth best weapon against communist propaganda. *U.S. Army.*

●   ●   ●

I find Martensen on the shady side of the building, puffing on his pipe and reading *The Centurions.* He glances up. "How did you do?"

"Oh, I suppose I missed a couple, but I made out. How about you?"

"I think maybe it was too easy. What took you so long to finish?"

"When I turned in my paper, Captain Le Boeuf called me upstairs to ask again about staying on as an instructor. Let's walk over and get some coffee."

He stands and brushes off his fatigues. "What did you tell him?"

"Pretty much the same thing we told him the other

day. I came to Special Forces to learn, not to teach. I want to get on to branch training and cross-training and get to the field."

Martensen grunts his approval. Reed has preceded us to the snack bar and waves as we enter.

"What were you trying to do," I ask, "set a new track record for examinations?"

He smiles. "I couldn't sit still any longer, so when I went back over it and I started getting doubts, I said to hell with it and turned it in. I passed. Where's Brulet?"

"The last I saw of him," I answer, "he was still working and complaining to the proctor about the wording of some of the questions. I guess except for getting our grades and turning in our manuals, that's it."

Reed pours another cup of coffee. "I checked; we definitely start branch on Monday."

I turn to Martensen. "I've been talking with Ted Mott and from what he says branch is really going to be a drag. Most of the stuff they're teaching we've already learned, and except for counterinsurgency and working with people with different MOSs, it's just something to be endured."

"I've heard the same thing, but at least it has some field work. While you're up, get me some more iced tea."

When I get back, Reed is saying, ". . . and another thing, it certainly eliminates the five-o'clock soldier. Half of the NCOs who came in with Duncan and me are long gone. Why do you suppose most of them quit, Dunc?"

"For a lot of reasons—financial hardship, the PCS thing, tired of changing barracks twice a week, illness at home. Many of them thought that most of the training was going to be outdoor stuff, not classroom work and homework, and they didn't like being schoolboys."

"Right!" Reed almost pounces. "But all those words

add up to one thing—non-professional. They aren't stupid or without talent, but they don't have the proper frame of mind for professional soldiers. They want an eight-to-five job. Financial hardships? We all have those—it sort of goes with the rank. They get a phone call from home and immediately run to help. What would they do on a mission? They should be ashamed to be NCOs. The Army comes first and family second, but most of them haven't the guts to make plain to their wives that what's good for the Army is good for them. What's a little inconvenience? Like coming to Special Forces. I didn't ask my wife for permission—she wouldn't expect it. When I make myself a better soldier, it helps the Army. If I'm a better soldier, I'll be promoted. The Army pays the bills. It's all very simple—take care of the Army; it will take care of you."

Martensen and I nod in agreement. He's right, of course.

AN HOUR BEFORE DAWN the company halts and the Vietnamese leader positions the two American NCOs and their interpreter in a brush thicket. The pre-dawn air is cold against the ambushers' sweaty bodies, a result of the all-night forced march.

With the arrival of full light come the sounds of a creaking cart pulled by a snuffling, heavily plodding buffalo. Those in the ambush tense when they hear male voices chattering.

Before the owners of the voices come into view the morning birds are stilled by a shrill command. *"Dung lai! Gio tay len!"*—"Halt! Raise your hands!"

A high-pitched voice shouts, *"Dung le ban! Dung le ban!"*—"Don't shoot!"

In their green and black tiger-striped suits the men cautiously stand and move toward the disturbance. The two NCOs welcome the chance to stretch and rid themselves of the ants. When they join the others, they find soldiers, guns pointed, standing over four prisoners who squat quietly, hands clasped behind their heads. Two wear homemade go-aheads * and two are barefooted; all wear the flyless black shorts which serve Vietnamese men as outer and under garment, and their shirts have age

* Similar to rubber sandal-type shower slippers.

and lack of laundering in common. One man, obviously frightened, is on the verge of tears; two stare sullenly at the ground; the fourth is openly angry and defiant.

The Vietnamese leader fires sharp questions at the men and hears *"thoi"*—"no" or *"khong co"*—"none" from three but only tight-lipped silence from the fourth.

The interpreter whispers to the Americans, "They say they not VC. They say they have not seen any and do not know where any are."

The questions get louder. The stocky commander, angered by the stubborn silence of the one man, suddenly pulls out his .45 pistol and points it into the defiant face, angrily repeating a question. The young man's answering tone matches his inquisitor's, and he doesn't restrict himself to a monosyllable. A heavy cuff across the head sends him sprawling. Without hesitation he resumes his squatting position and glares at his tormentor, who unexpectedly bursts into laughter and holsters his pistol. He turns his back on the four men and issues a string of orders.

The men are relieved of their ID cards and loaded with sundry equipment—one shoulders the machine gun, another the heavy communal cooking pot and a sack of rice; the defiant man is given two metal boxes of machine-gun ammunition, and the fourth is loaded with a radio and extra ammo. They are to be taken along as suspects.

The company is broken into three platoons and with the suspects in the center column, they move out under the heat of the rising sun. After an hour of moving across the open, flat rice country the center platoon arrives at a paddy where an old man is turning the soil with a crude plow. In response to a shouted order the old man leaves his terrified wife and approaches the Vietnamese leader. He keeps bowing, hands pressed together, in the prayer-like manner of the Buddhists, and each time he bends his wispy chin whiskers almost touch his walnut-brown legs. Neither his obsequiousness nor his wife's pleading wails prevent him from being pressed into service as a suspect. As the sun grows hotter and the loads heavier, other suspects are added and by noon there are eleven.

The platoons come together for the two-hour noon break and a quick lunch. The soldiers stretch out and the suspects squat a short distance away in an attitude of resigned patience. The commander, standing in the scanty shade of a scrub tree, says something to his platoon leader whose mouth twists in a grin. The platoon leader walks over to the prisoners, yanks the old man to his feet, and shoves him forward, almost throwing him on his face. White head bobbing, the old man shuffles forward, hands again together in obeisance. The grinning platoon leader follows. The commander shouts at the lowered head, smiles, and points to the ground. When the old farmer doesn't move fast enough, the leader sends him sprawling with a blow from his fist, never losing his smile, and sits down beside him. When he starts to sit up, a hard push against his bony chest flings him back down.

One of the sergeants starts to get up but is stopped by his sidekick. "Sit down. He's only going to ask him some questions. He knows what he's doing."

"I doubt it," the other answers. "That's no way to treat a subject for interrogation."

"Relax—and don't interfere."

"But he shouldn't be questioning him in front of the others. Even if the old guy knows something, which I doubt, he's not going to volunteer anything in front of the others. If he's forced to talk and the others hear it, it will be his death warrant when the VC find out."

"Maybe that's the idea."

The sergeant, seated again, stares in disbelief at his companion. "You mean they're not even serious about information? It's a game?"

"Maybe. Maybe not. In any event, it's none of your business."

"By God, I'll make it mine. We've got to stop it."

"Now you listen. We don't 'got' to do anything and we won't. This is your first time out; you'll keep your mouth shut and watch—and keep your opinions to yourself." He looks long and levelly at his agitated friend.

"But . . ."

"But nothing. Shut up."

The commander stretches out alongside the old man and talks to him in a soothing voice. Each time the man raises his head it is slammed back to the ground. The eyes of the other suspects are on the pair on the ground. The defiant young man stares at the commander with naked unblinking hatred. The tormentor moves closer to his victim and, still smiling, moves as if to embrace him. Instead he yanks the old man's head back with one hand and pins the thrashing legs with his own. A hunting knife appears in the other hand.

The commander keeps his syrupy soothing tone as he pricks and scratches the farmer's neck and chest with the point of the blade. Abruptly, he lets the knife dent the skin under the chin whiskers and his voice changes to anger and impatience—a fraction more pressure on the blade and a bloody puncture is certain. Guttural sounds come from the distended leathery throat—the pressure is released.

The old man babbles, his torrents of words interrupted occasionally by sharp words from the knife-holder. Finally the commander pushes the bony frame aside, and stands, laughing. The old man, tears in his eyes, shuffles back to the other prisoners and squats, head bent, in utter dejection and desolation. The soldiers laugh in appreciation of the fine diversion.

For the first time the platoon leader notices the look of the one prisoner directed at the commander. He strides over and, swinging his carbine at the man's head, lays him flat.

The older sergeant again hauls his companion to the ground, saying, "Forget it."

"Forget it? That guy should be in jail."

"In jail? That's the best man we have! Don't make waves."

"But, Dick, we can't let him get away with it . . . either one of them. We've got to report this. They're not human."

"Look, I know how you feel, but you get used to it. See that thing around his neck that looks like an amulet? It was only a little more than a month ago that I . . ."

SERGEANT DUNCAN."

My head snaps up guiltily and I spin around to the hand on my shoulder. I've been drifting off again.

"An officer at the door wants to speak to you and Sergeant Martensen."

I stand and turn my back on the droning voice on the platform explaining for the third time about open and closed quadrants. Martensen precedes me down the aisle between the bored students. Captain Le Boeuf is waiting, his baggy shirt showing dark sweat stains.

"Sir?" I ask and salute.

His return salute is more like a hand wave. "Let's walk over to the shade. How do you like branch training?"

Martensen grunts. "It is very boring and very slow."

"I thought you would find it like that. I came by to ask you two to reconsider instructing for O and I. Frankly, we need you. We have a bigger class this cycle and two of our instructors will have to leave soon. We need people who can teach and who know the material. How about it?" He slaps me jovially on the shoulder.

"It's very flattering, sir, but I want to finish branch and get on to cross-training, and then to a permanent team. The sooner I get squared away, the sooner I can qualify for a PCS."

"What about you, Sergeant Martensen?"

"Same thing, sir. I want to get trained."

"Lookit, men, if that's your main worry, there's no problem. You can take the end-of-course examination and make a field trip and that's all you need for branch. It's mostly for the people with other MOSs anyway. Cross-training is nothing, a sort of hit-and-miss affair that doesn't come anywhere near MOS training. You'll just get started on say, demolitions, and you'll be pulled for ash and trash, sweeping streets, or some other nonsense. Stay with us and you can go to the other committees and get solid MOS training. This is the deal—the only time you have to be in the classroom is when you're teaching. As long as your classes are prepared you can spend the rest of your time at weapons training, commo, or whatever. You'll get better training faster than the people who go to the group. Say you'll do it, and I'll get PCS orders for you within ten days."

"Are you sure we can get the training when we want it?" I ask.

"I personally guarantee it. Many of the instructors float from committee to committee to keep up."

"All right, sir. I'll do it."

"Sergeant Martensen?"

He nods. "When do you want us to start?"

"Get your books and start right now. I'll phone ahead to say you're coming. I'll be along in an hour. Good luck —and thanks."

"I just hope we haven't been given a snow job, Jon. I hope this is the right move. How come you accepted?"

"Because I think what he says about better training this way is true. Also there are too many NCOs with our 113 MOS going into the groups who are E-7s. I am an

E-6, like you, which means I would not get my own team, and I wouldn't want to be on a team led by White or Harrison. I might even be promoted here and when I go to group I will be the best-trained E-7 team sergeant around."

The months pass. The teaching becomes routine after the first cycle, requiring little or no preparation. Originally scheduled for Tactical Terrain Studies and Interrogation Techniques, I soon inherit Fingerprinting and Photography.

A couple of cycles after we started, Special Forces began to get more operations and intelligence NCOs than there were teams to put them on, so we taught only every second cycle, which was ideal for our training.

In communications we learned Morse code at a speed of better than twice the five words per minute required for cross-training. We quit when we found that because of a shortage of qualified men, those showing a capability for more than fifteen words were being converted to full-time radio operators.

We took the full weapons course and for the first time I fired one of the new Colt Armelite AR-15s—and fell in love with it. Special Forces was trying to talk the Army into adopting this new weapon, but they were having difficulties—too practical, we decided. For Martensen, an old Infantryman, the course was a snap, but I had some problems with the mortar since I had never used one. The foreign weapons were diverse and interesting—we marveled at the German MG-42 machine gun and regarded the U.S. M-60 an inferior copy.

We started Demolitions/Engineering with a certain amount of trepidation, since it had a notorious washout rate—one class graduated two out of forty students—and as well-established instructors, we would have been embarrassed to make a bad showing. But we had no cause for alarm—both of us finished with higher grades in Demo than in O and I. It was a fascinating course—non-electric and electric circuits, conventional demo, blowing bridges, booby traps, grenade ambushes; ear muff, platter diamond, triangle and ribbon charges; homemade shotguns; making black powder and our own incendiaries, time bombs from tin cans, homemade claymores and explosives and incendiaries from kitchen chemicals.

The chief instructor for Demo explained the reason for the washout rate: "It's the math that gets 'em, and we get sent more than our fair share of niggers. They just can't cut it. Some of them come here and they can't even do long division with decimals." He added rather proudly, "We graduate fewer coons than any other committee, and usually we don't even have to red line them —we discourage them into quitting."

Medical training, my first choice when I came to Special Forces, had to be picked up whenever opportunity permitted. We would slip over to the dog lab at the hospital to watch the advanced enlisted students practicing surgery—their first operation was usually on the dog's larynx, thereby rendering the patient barkless for future surgery. Sometimes the dog had to be shot so the student could learn the debridement of gunshot wounds. The students doted on the dogs, hovering over them for endless hours, and the death of a patient usually meant the end of medical training for the "doctor." I was amazed at the young men's competence and dedication, and I envied their skill but couldn't take the fifty weeks necessary for the full training.

●　●　●

During my teaching period one of the most significant events pertaining to the future character of Special Forces occurred, and for the first time, something took precedence over training (training, incidentally, that was never made up). Every enlisted man and officer on Smoke Bomb Hill was affected: men were detailed to build floats, the Psychological Warfare Battalion cranked out millions of leaflets and painted huge posters and backdrops, engineers were detailed to drive huge logs into the mud of McKellar's Lake and support them with cables. Strange equipment appeared. Mock submarines were knocked together. Speeches were written and rehearsed, rewritten and rehearsed again. Sky divers practiced jumping into the lake, others practiced jumping into the trees behind the lake. Mock battles, complete with ambushes, were rehearsed. A team with a "Rube Goldberg" rocket belt appeared. Hundreds of NCOs spent countless man-hours picking up bits of paper along the road leading to the lake. Then it was mass rehearsals from morning to night —talkthroughs, walkthroughs, and, finally, dress rehearsals. This had to be a real Cecil B. De Mille spectacular. President Kennedy was coming!

It was a dazzling show and certainly worth the thousands of dollars and thousands of man-hours. First came the floats depicting the facets of Special Warfare. Then a twelve-man "A" team complete with rucksacks and weapons, each man explaining his job, cross-training, and other skills, and testifying to his ability to speak some exotic language. Each man wore the forbidden Green Beret.*

* Shortly after Special Forces started wearing the beret in the fifty's it was copied by other units—paratroopers, tankers, etc. To stop the tendency toward "private armies," the order forbidding the beret for all was issued.

A LARK (a small amphibious lighter) lumbered into the lake, carrying a man wearing the rocket contraption —jets roaring, he flew across the water and landed in front of the President. Scuba divers swam to shore from the dummy submarine; skydivers trailing colored smoke tracked in from fifteen thousand feet and hit the water as planned; an expert judo team brutally displayed their skills; another group climbed the tall poles and made thrilling rides on a "slide-for-life" * into the water. The ambush went off without a hitch—low-level passes were made with L-19s, Caribous, Mohawks, and helicopters; on cue over a thousand men who had been hiding in the brush across the lake stood and removed fatigue shirts, and in their white T-shirts, shooting off hand flares, ran screaming and yelling to the water's edge. They represented the number of guerrillas the twelve-man team can organize and direct. Hundreds of men from the Seventh appeared elsewhere on the lake—all wearing the forbidden beret. The message is clear: these are the skills that every Special Forces man has. We are ready to go. We are yours. Use us. Then millions of leaflets drop over the area—they are printed with the President's picture.

When it is over I glance at Martensen, who is frowning in deep thought. So few qualified men were around that the judo and "slide-for-life" demonstration teams were imported from the Ranger School at Fort Benning;

* A long rope or cable is run from the top of a pole on the far bank at a sharp angle to a body of water. A hand pulley is slipped over the rope and the rider hangs on while it runs swiftly to the water. Body weight makes the rope flatten slightly near the bank and the rider picks up his feet, hitting the water at a shallow angle but at great speed. Ostensibly, a way to cross a stream, it is actually more of a confidence-course gimmick.

scuba-qualified people could be counted on a couple of hands. Much of the equipment shown, including the rocket, had never been seen before and probably would never be seen again, and much of it had no application to Special Forces anyway. The fancy rappelling had also been done by non-Special Forces personnel; the typical twelve-man "A" team had been picked from as many teams for the occasion. If German, French, and Spanish were excluded, those in Special Forces who spoke foreign languages were a fractional minority.

We had witnessed one of the most magnificent, impressive, bald-faced, complex, and expensive snow jobs ever. But it wasn't for nothing: President Kennedy told General Yarborough and the men of Special Forces to ". . . wear the beret proudly; it will be a mark of distinction and a badge of courage . . ."

It was now legal to wear the heretofore forbidden Green Beret.

●　　●　　●

Even before the last leaflets were picked up Special Forces—with the President's blessing—was no longer a poor cousin to the 82nd Airborne Division or the XVIII Airborne Corps; and while the "regulars" bit their collective lips, Special Forces moved fast to consolidate their position. The United States Army Center for Special Warfare gained relative autonomy and direct lines to the main man, and almost overnight everything enlarged—a classic in the art of empire building. When I entered Special Forces, it consisted of the First Group in Okinawa, the Seventh Group at Fort Bragg, and the Tenth Group in Germany; all were under strength, never had enough money (hence everyone had to scrounge and improvise, which gave rise to the nickname "Sneaky Petes"), and had terrible promotion possibilities.

Now the Fifth Group was activated at Bragg, the provisional training company became the Training Group, and not much later the Eighth Group was activated and sent to Panama. Spanish-Americans and others fluent in Spanish were soon to see service, in covert and overt roles, in a growing number of Central and South American countries. The following year the Third and Sixth Groups were activated.

Smoke Bomb Hill, the home of a little-known and exclusive club, became overcrowded and spilled across the highway into the reserve training area. An organization which had shunned publicity, it now employed every Madison Avenue technique to create and perpetuate an image. The Psychological Warfare Battalions were enlarged and made part of the center, and the Propaganda and Leaflet Companies put out posters, books, and pamphlets at high speed. It became a joke that the twelve-man A team had been enlarged, like the Marines, to include a photographer for the public information office. "Disneyland," the elaborate demonstration area, was so well used to impress visiting politicians, Boy Scouts, Military Brass, foreign dignitaries, and the public at large that men were assigned on an almost permanent basis to operate it; eventually, an even more elaborate "Disneyland" was built, thereby creating a site for a huge new Center for Special Warfare. Teams were organized to fly around the country to put on shows for the public. Because of the influx of foreign officers, special kitchens served foods strange to the average American palate.

During this growth period all teams were officially withdrawn from Laos, but added commitments in Viet-

Nam and Latin America more than offset this move. Teams from the First Group in Okinawa were starting to meet themselves coming and going to Viet-Nam, and the Tenth in Germany—low in priority—was being stripped due to lack of replacements. In Washington special liaison people were on permanent duty, and staffs burgeoned at all levels. As more and more students streamed in, a proportionate number of instructors had to be pulled from teams. People had to be assigned to disburse the money for equipment and training that poured in. The structure was growing but so were commitments, and the away-from-home groups felt the pressure. As Special Forces grew, so did the ratio of staff personnel to field teams.

Stripes for NCOs flooded in at such a rate that it sometimes was difficult to find people to promote; this attracted large numbers of NCOs who saw Special Forces as a fast road to promotion, and soon it was come one, come all. Classes went on double shift and the programs expanded, but the spectacular washout rate indicated that many of the newcomers had not been promoted in their old units for good reasons. New young soldiers, enchanted by the PR image and the romanticism of the beret, also were attracted by the publicity. Unfortunately, the mentality that brought them to Special Forces was the same that had made them high school dropouts, and as admissions standards were lowered, the number of misfits, malcontents, and those unwanted by their old outfits increased.

Washington became upset over the money being spent to ship men from all over the country to Fort Bragg just to have them fail (in one demolitions training class of forty men only one passed). Regular Brass refused to believe that such a large percentage of men in the Regular Army were academically unqualified and decided that the fault lay with inferior instruction. A team of investigators from George Washington University was dispatched to Fort Bragg, and while they found no fault with the instruction, they did find that many men had come only to get away from their own units while others lacked the dedication that Reed had discussed in the coffee shop. Some were disillusioned when they found that reality did not match the recruiting posters. Something had to be done.

It was made more difficult to fail a student for academic reasons, but when it was unavoidable, the student was recycled, sometimes in a different course, sometimes in the same one; some were given third chances, and some were passed on even if they failed. As a single example, one NCO failed the O and I course in spite of off-duty coaching; recycled to weapons training, he failed that and was sent back to O and I, where, though he knew the solutions to the assignments, he fell far short of a passing grade. I met him in Viet-Nam in 1964 —he was a Special Forces intelligence sergeant.

Shortly after the buildup got underway, Special Forces men were sent to Africa, Asia, Latin America, and Europe, which meant in some cases that assignments were made to Okinawa and elsewhere before branch or cross-training was completed. It wasn't long before the First Group in Okinawa complained that many of the people they were receiving were so poorly trained they had to retrain them, further burdening already extended facilities.

It was deduced that those best qualified for Special Forces would also be the more valuable people in other organizations. It was assumed that since no commander likes to see his best men leave, the applications of the better personnel were sidetracked or disapproved and the less qualified men were being sent. This assumption and the approval of the Continental Army Command resulted in the formation of a Special Forces Procurement Program—the empire grows. Senior NCOs from the Fifth, Seventh, and Training Groups were to be sent to key installations in the United States with virtual *carte blanche* to accept men for training. These NCOs probably were not going to be the most popular men on their assigned posts.

●   ●   ●

I was sitting in the Group Headquarters, completing a jumpmaster's report from the previous day's jump, when the group commander and his executive officer walked past.

"Major, we've got to come up with one more name—Center is screaming. It seems nobody wants to volunteer . . . Hello, Sergeant Duncan. You know anybody who might be interested?"

"In what, sir?"

"Being a Special Forces recruiter. It was all on a memorandum sent to each committee."

"First I heard of it, sir. What's it all about?"

The commander turned with a smile to the XO. "Now we know why no volunteers. The committee chiefs don't want to lose any of their instructors." Shaking his head, he turned back to me. "Can you think of someone who might do it?"

"Yes, sir," I replied impulsively. "Me."

"You? Who will teach your classes?"

"We're out of cycle right now and I'm just filling time, teaching rappelling and rope bridges to pre-students. Besides, since I've been spending more time on field trips than I have on the podium for the last few months, I have a competent understudy."

"Sir," the XO said, "this may be our answer. Center wants somebody in thirty minutes and we can't hold Sergeant Duncan in group much longer; he's already been here longer than most of the other instructors."

"Okay, Sergeant Duncan, report to the captain in the adjutant's office at Center Headquarters. They're interviewing applicants right now. We'll call and let them know you're coming."

It was hard to believe that after all my attempts, Training Group was actually going to let me leave. Seven or eight applicants were exchanging light banter with a captain when I arrived.

"Are you Sergeant Duncan?"

"Yes, sir."

"Come into my office."

Inside, I reported and sat down in the proffered chair.

"Why do you want to be a recruiter, Sergeant?"

"Sir, I'm an instructor in Training Group. I have seen the steady decrease in quality of people we are getting for training, and if Special Forces are to remain 'special,' we must find a higher caliber of student. I'm not only one of the older instructors in group, I have also been through every MOS course taught here. I have worked directly with the demo committee and the branch committee. I know the problems, what kind of people are needed, and who can handle the training." I was impressed with my speech but had neglected to mention that I was restless and felt I had to get away from what had become a routine job, even if it meant becoming a recruiter.

"Thank you, Sergeant. That will be all."

Puzzled by the one-question interview, I joined the

others in the hall. The paunchy captain walked out behind me and anounced that those present were accepted and were to report for briefing the following morning.

Briefings in administrative procedures were followed by a dress rehearsal of the pitch before General Yarborough, who then addressed us. The gist was that the procurement program was designed to cut back the input through our screening and eliminating personnel at the source, thus guaranteeing a greater output of high-caliber graduates; fewer cadre would be required to produce more trained personnel. Although they hoped for more, it was all right if we sent one man a month, as long as he was qualified and could make it through the training: "I want good, dedicated men who will graduate. If you want him, take him. Just remember, he may be on your team someday."

Final instructions from the captain in charge of the program were more succinct: "Don't send me any niggers. Be careful, however, not to give the impression that we are prejudiced in Special Forces. You won't find it hard to find an excuse to reject them; most will be too dumb to pass the written test. If they luck out on that and get by the physical testing, you'll find they have some sort of police record. Remember, you don't have to give anybody a reason for not accepting him, even if he passes all the tests. The interview is the most important part of the screening. Just ask yourself, 'Would I want him on my team?' "

I wondered what General Yarborough would have thought of that. Some of the old-timers in Special Forces blamed the General for what they thought was its ruin —they deplored the fast buildup, the lowering of standards, the end of exclusiveness, the publicity, the destruction of eliteness except in name. Some said he was using

Special Forces as a means of collecting stars, but nobody ever suggested he was prejudiced. Even those with real or imagined grievances against him talked of him as a good family man, a man who had carried himself well in time of personal tragedy and who placed high value on personal morality. To some he seemed an odd choice to be the commander of an organization who, because of a propensity for back-door adventures,* added daily to their reputation as "Sneaky Petes." Knowledge of such behavior was cause for immediate dismissal by the General, as were letters of indebtedness, passing bad checks, and unseemly conduct off post. Thus it seemed unlikely that a man with such high standards would pick an officer with such prejudices to head a worldwide procurement program.

●　　●　　●

I was assigned to the California area, and Fort Ord, on the Monterey Peninsula, was my base of operations. The area has an atmosphere (despite the number of retired colonels, generals, and admirals) quite different from that surrounding Southern military posts—the result, I think, of the natural beauty, the traditions of the permanent citizens, and the lack of Southern tradition, chauvinism, and prejudice. Whatever it is, the newcomer has an almost irresistible urge to create and give of himself—a very unmilitary trait—and people who stay for any length of time want to paint, write, play an instrument, or at least engage in philosophical dialogue. I found myself eventually spending more time in discussion and in reading books not connected with the Military.

* A name coined as a result of men walking in the back door while husbands were off on missions.

I was joined the first week on the post by the captain (who arrived via Nevada three days late, looking a little grubbier than usual). We proceeded to make the rounds of the area's major post headquarters, where the captain briefed majors and colonels on what was "special" about Special Forces. Skeptical eyebrows were raised at the disparity between his words and his appearance.

At each stop he made a point of stressing that we wouldn't take many Negroes, ". . . not because we're prejudiced, you understand, but because they usually aren't suitable. Motivation for a Negro volunteer is usually quite different. They think the beret is 'Cool, man.' Besides, there are only certain places we can use them, since in many places they would be too conspicuous. Authorities of some of the governments we work with have asked us not to send any."

This came as news to me. Considering that the sudden expansion was for counterinsurgency, particularly in Viet-Nam, it was difficult to see how a Negro would be any more conspicuous than a white, especially now that Special Forces were wearing American uniforms in that country. I still have no idea of the truth of the statement, but if it is true, it gives a rather alarming insight into the types of government our country supports.

Three or four times a week for fifteen months I spoke to groups of a hundred soldiers, of whom an average of ten would come into my office. Usually, after processing and investigation, one was accepted.

It wasn't long before the captain called from Fort Bragg. I was averaging four or five men a week—a figure I was rather proud of since it was far above the one qualified man per month we had been told about at the briefing—and we had been told there was no quota; now, I was informed, they wanted twenty-five to thirty men a week. Since the source of men and the amount of time necessary to process them was unchanged, waivers were granted for not quite qualified men and processing time was cut. Ultimately, clerks handled the processing and I saw a man only at a short final interview. The result of all this was not a decrease in input and an increase in output, but the opposite; problems at the Special Warfare Center remained the same, and only the captain's charts indicated a job well done. Work continued. Pressures were put on to get more and more people. I learned that very few of the West Coast draftees were impressed with the "line-'em-up, shine-'em-up, RA all the way" sales pitch. To the horror of the "regular" cadre, I often showed up on the stage in Levis and a baggy sweater to deliver a very subtle non-military pitch to a hundred basic trainees. It was a little misleading for the recruits who swarmed into my office, but a quota is a quota.

The rest of my job was public relations. When I first came to California wearing my Green Beret, I was continually mistaken for a foreign soldier or, as some wags had it, "a member of the Carmel National Guard." It was necessary to sell Special Forces to the public and to the Army, and I became a familiar sight at Rotary and Lions Clubs and at Boy Scout meetings. On special occasions I arranged for demonstration teams, and I made a point of being interviewed frequently by the local papers. I gave Troop Information classes and worked closely with recruiters. I was only one of many scattered around the country to stump for "Kennedy's Own."

So successful was the Special Forces' PR campaign that it not only survived the death of its biggest booster, John F. Kennedy, and the inter-service resentment of the "regulars," but actually continued to grow. We weren't a hard product to sell, and the American public was ready

—so today there are a best-selling book, record, and comic strip about the Green Berets and the glories of war, Green Beret dolls, and a Green Beret exercise book. John Wayne, that professional non-soldier soldier, will produce and star in his version of Robin Moore's book—the only recruiting pamphlet to make the best-seller list.

For ten dollars Sears will send you a Special Forces outpost, complete with machine gun, rifle, hand grenades, rockets, field telephone, and two plastic Green Beret soldiers. Montgomery Ward's Christmas catalogue offers, for five dollars, ". . . a uniform designed for rugged Green Beret duty . . . to see tough little soldiers through many a fray . . . in all your around-the-world jobs for the Special Forces . . ." and to help celebrate the birthday of the Prince of Peace, they will send along, for an additional six dollars, a "Green Beret Combat Set," which includes an AR-15 rifle (Sears' looks more realistic but isn't as big), a pistol, a fliptop military holster, and, of course, a beret; sorry, no caps included. For those in the lower-income brackets there is "Men of the Green Berets" bubble gum (five cents), in addition to which you receive four cards depicting the art of killing (save enough cards and the backs make up a picture puzzle); the important thing about this package is its message: "Start your own A team! Wear the Green Beret . . . Send only five Green Beret bubble gum wrappers and 60¢ with your name, address, and zip code . . ."

● ● ●

And so another generation is prepared to walk unresistingly into the ovens of war.

SPECIAL FORCES' mission at its inception was to infiltrate trained guerrillas into foreign countries to teach indigenous populations how to mount insurrections against unpopular governments. The Russians, it was said, were only waiting for an opportune moment to overrun Western Europe and push the free-world forces into the Atlantic. The regular forces would then fight a delaying battle back along their lines of communication and withdraw from Germany, while additional forces would be sent and a consolidated stand would be made at the sea. The free-world forces would shorten their communication lines and the communists would be forced to extend theirs. As soon as the first shot was fired, Special Forces would jump in at predetermined places behind the advancing communists. After so many years of communist domination there would obviously be overwhelming popular dissatisfaction, and it would be a simple matter to organize, equip, and train the people; the insurrection would force the communist forces to divert more and more troops from the front, thereby relieving pressure on the regulars.

During the fifties and early sixties the Strategic Air Command expanded enormously; more and more bases were built on the periphery of the free world, and tactical and strategic nuclear weapons were sent to Europe to provide for immediate and massive retaliation. The need for Special Forces steadily diminished, though there were awkward moments—like Hungary. (Can nuclear weapons be used discriminately? If ground troops were not sufficient to hold the line against the communist forces, how could we have moved into Hungary? We could have dropped the bomb on Russia, but how would they have retaliated?)

Special Forces obviously would never be deployed according to the original plan. The future was grim, for there had never been enthusiastic support in the Army for this bunch of strange people. In the late fifties the CIA and others used limited numbers in Viet-Nam, but primarily to teach conventional subjects to the Vietnamese Rangers and the CIDG Strike Forces. A field-grade commander assigned to an organization with no function in the overall scheme of things either develops a function or faces a dead end.

Did Special Forces expand so rapidly because the Russians were ready to roll across Western Europe? Of course not. Assuming that a group is at full strength, it would theoretically be able to organize 240,000 guerrillas. The British experience in Malaya taught that it takes a ratio of ten to one to put down an insurrection; thus the enemy would have to divert almost two and a half million troops to offset the work of one Special Forces group.

The reason for the sudden growth was that a new commander found a new function in the overall scheme: counterinsurgency; primary target: Viet-Nam. It wasn't easy to sell, especially to the regulars, the idea of Special Forces as counterinsurgents. Counterinsurgency is basically a conventional military operation involving such time-tested tactics as encirclement and the hammer-and-anvil concept. (Our Indian Wars are examples of conventional forces successfully employed against a guerrilla force.)

Who, the argument developed, is better qualified to fight guerrillas—conventional forces or men trained as guerrillas? Who can anticipate guerrilla moves better than someone thoroughly familiar with the psychology and doctrine of guerrilla warfare? Who is better able to "win the hearts and minds of the people" than a man trained to work with indigenous personnel? The best people to fight guerrillas are other guerrillas—anti-guerrillas. And—the clincher—if we use the Vietnamese, we can gain our ends in Viet-Nam without committing large numbers of American troops, thereby making it acceptable to the American people.

Jumping channels, showmanship, infusions of money, endless strategy meetings, and politicking had their way, and Special Forces—which had been in danger of joining the Rangers and the Commandos—had a job and a new definition: "Defenders of freedom's frontiers."

To the already immense American legions, those in uniform and those in society conditioned by the uniformed military, a new legion is added. Essentially professional and composed of older men, it will strive to be a Praetorian guard to preserve Corpus Americanus, and because they are professional, their primary loyalty will be to their fatherland: the legion. Their battle cry: Anti-Communism; their motto: To Liberate from Oppression.

● ● ●

Counterinsurgency is not just fighting guerrillas, any more than insurgency is arming a group to fight. Insurgency is political, a popular uprising against a govern-

ment—to overthrow the leaders (a revolt) or to change
the form of government (a revolution). In revolution
especially, armed conflict is not an essential but normally
comes after the elimination of due process to achieve
desired political goals, and even then overt guerrilla action is only one part of the political movement. Counterinsurgency must exist both to defeat the guerrillas and
to consider the causes of the insurgency, and it can choose
to respond by changing the leaders and the form of government; convincing the people that they are mistaken
and that the existing government is good for them; or
convincing the people that the government proposed by
the insurgents would make things worse for them.

To relate the first choice to Viet-Nam: Our admission
of the necessity for counterinsurgency was *prima facie*
evidence of an existing insurgency, and it provided proof
that the government and its leaders had no intention
of changing voluntarily. If we are to believe our own
propaganda, we were in Viet-Nam by invitation of the
government (the same government that had eliminated
due process), not to change it, but to maintain it. Propaganda aside, since we had created and financed the
government in the first place, it could be said that we
invited ourselves; and since the government developed
as it had under our aegis, it would seem obvious that
serious change was not to be part of the program. In any
event, for an outside power to step in and make the
change would accomplish nothing, because it was outside intervention and interference in Vietnamese affairs
that had started the trouble. Special Forces personnel
are taught not to interfere in internal politics when organizing the guerrillas because it would create resentment. Why, then, should we have supposed that interference in internal politics while fighting against the

guerrillas would be any less resented? (Mark well that in this period we were talking of insurgency; it would be a few years before the American people could swallow "invasion.")

The second response poses equally interesting problems. How could outsiders, for the most part incapable of fully understanding the people to whom they are appealing, convince the people that what they regarded as evil was really good? The outsiders' values were different but not necessarily better—their history is unique to them and they have never lived under such a government; their opposition is Vietnamese talking to Vietnamese. (The task of an outsider in a country which has just gained independence from a colonial power is more difficult.)

One course was to initiate civic action programs, which again offered two alternatives: the Vietnamese government could handle these programs or the Americans could. There is a large disparity between the amounts spent on arms and on civic action, and a similar imbalance between the amount earmarked for civic action and that which finally reaches the people. Aid to unpopular governments is invariably used to strengthen the government, and when a significant segment of the population has lost faith in a government's honesty and integrity, watching officials pocket money intended for the people can only increase their contempt. Americans handling the programs were just that—the people do not identify the action with the government—and it was further proof that the government could not be trusted. And what could it do for the Americans? In a country that believes that a man who gives something for nothing is a fool, not asking for something in return could be interpreted as an attempt to buy love or acceptance of American ways—or it could mean that the American is a fool. In a country where the people survived for generations by learning to tell outsiders what they wanted to hear, how can the outsider determine whether he is thought of as an opportunist capitalizing on others' misery, or a fool, or both?

It is utterly unreasonable to try to convince people who in desperation have taken arms against the government that a change, any change, can worsen things, for at this stage they are convinced that things cannot get worse and that even vague promises hold more hope than day-to-day reality. Political opposition, communist and non-communist, had been eliminated, the leaders hunted down or chased from the country. An army of security police crawled across Viet-Nam, seeking out all those who dared voice disapproval of the regime; portable guillotines moved from village to village to expedite summary justice, and the jails were filled with political prisoners dying under the most barbaric circumstances. The armed forces were being used as tax collectors and to protect the government and landlords from the people. Peasants who thought they had won their land in their fight for independence were forced to pay for it or see it returned to the landlords. The black market, fed by American largesse and government corruption, enriched a few while the rest grew poorer. Elections, though an unopposed mockery, were rigged. How could outsiders —well fed, well clothed, with an excess of money, living in air-conditioned hotels and villas, cooperating with the government responsible for the conditions—convince people living in a nightmare that the other guys were worse? It turned out to be far easier to convince the American people that Vietnamese communists were trying to take over a free country—and that this was the worst thing possible—than it was to convince the Vietnamese of anything.

It is a testimonial to our media and propagandists that unable to define "communism," the American people know it is EVIL; and unable to define "democracy," know it is GOOD. Generations of experience with Chinese, French, Portuguese, Japanese, and now American propaganda taught the Vietnamese how to listen, nod, and then compare propaganda against performance—as a result, they have developed the irrational notion that what is good or bad for the United States is not necessarily good or bad for Viet-Nam.

Propaganda does not necessarily mean "lies," of course, and all governments, agencies, and organizations use it. The U.S. Army defines propaganda as ". . . any information, ideas, doctrines, or special appeals disseminated to influence the opinions, emotions, attitudes of any specified group in order to benefit the sponsor . . ." The first two words and the last four are particularly significant. Truth is likely to be the best propaganda, but it is not necessarily the most effective. Effectiveness of propaganda is determined by the sponsor's understanding of the target audience. In selling Americans a doctrine, a candidate, or a detergent, American propagandists—who live with and in America, and who have analyzed, computerized, and tested their audience—have no peer. It is becoming more painfully apparent every year, however, that in foreign countries the same appeals often fall flat unless their interests coincide with ours.

Since they are Vietnamese, living with and in Viet-Nam, the forces arrayed against Saigon have the same advantages as Madison Avenue working in America. Propaganda devised by Americans, based on American beliefs and interests, when disseminated to a Vietnamese audience, can draw a response opposite to its purpose. For example: A village chief has been assassinated. Immediately, a pamphlet describing this act of terror is cranked out and widely distributed as one more proof of communist perfidy, the pamphleteers assuming that they and their audience agree as to what constitutes an act of terror. If the village chief was a Saigon appointee, he was probably living apart from the other villagers and exploiting them as well, and giving the communists credit for ridding the people of an unpopular official only strengthens their belief that only the NLF can bring changes; at best, the pamphlet demonstrates the government's inability to prevent such acts. In 1965 I saw a pamphlet describing how the NLF had blown up a bus on a Southern road—that Saigon did not control the road was not news, but distributing leaflets to brag about it hardly seemed necessary.

In 1961 Special Forces elements had been in Viet-Nam for some time but on a very minor scale. The problems confronting them, while not necessarily insurmountable, certainly were staggering. Had many of the plans for overcoming the problems been effected and carried through in 1955 and 1956, the chances of success would have been excellent; but then, of course, the insurgency would never have developed. What had begun as scattered political dissatisfaction evolved in the interim into a well-organized armed insurrection, implementing many of the programs the regime should have used in the areas they controlled. If a government accepts the old-fashioned idea that it exists for the people, it can institute radical reforms to stop a brewing rebellion short of bloody repression; but there is a point at which only the application of overwhelming force can put down a revolution. By 1961 Viet-Nam had reached that point, and there was going to be a lag time before Special Forces could be expanded sufficiently to implement a program.

No one knows why, but the guidelines chosen for a program were adopted from the British experience in Malaya. Aside from the vast political differences between Viet-Nam and Malaya, there were other major dissimilarities. The British never made any pretense of being guests in Malaya; they made it plain from the very beginning that they wanted to "unload," and one of their first moves was to tell the government to shape up or else. Having been in Malaya for years, they were familiar with the country and the people. The Malays had not just finished fighting and winning a bloody war of independence. The country did not have an artificial dividing line drawn through the middle, and no outside power was determined to make two countries out of one. At a very early stage the British instituted radical reforms to undermine the insurgents' appeal, resettled large numbers of peasants in protectable areas (the Strategic Hamlet concept), and used Special Air Service (SAS) teams in hit-and-run tactics directly against the guerrillas to great advantage.*

We have no way of knowing whether the opinion is valid that in Viet-Nam the best people to fight guerrillas are other guerrillas; to date it hasn't been tried. Special

* The SAS is organized along the small-team concept, but unlike Special Forces, they do the job themselves. Trained as small commando-type teams, not to train or advise or organize, they are not dependent on counterparts or on the loyalty and effectiveness of trained locals. Extremely efficient in their work, they realize that it would take years, not a six- or eight-week program, to train others on a mass basis to their degree of effectiveness. Although many people would like to be able to do this type of work, relatively few have the necessary natural skills, intelligence, cold-bloodedness, motivation, dedication, spirit, animal aggressiveness, and cunning.

Forces enlarged the CIDG program, which means that the people they trained were essentially minority ethnic groups within the country, such as the Montagnards. These so-called Strike Forces did not live off the land; their food was supplied. They lived not in villages but in camps surrounded by barbed wire and land mines —and since they lived in camps that had to be protected, they lacked the mobility of guerrillas and could never stray far. Their weapons were not captured but given to them, and the camps and the Strikers were actually an additional source of weaponry for the enemy. Their pay and allowances usually exceeded the regular forces', and because they were mercenaries—seldom recruited by ideological appeals, and exempt from army conscription—their loyalty to Saigon was doubtful. They were trained and deployed as conventional small units, not as guerrillas, and their training usually lasted only six to eight weeks before they went on a "live" action. The "A" team within the camp lived separate from the Strikers and their LLDB counterparts, and the LLDB kept apart, for seldom was any love lost between the ethnic Vietnamese and the *"moîs"*—savages—as the Vietnamese called them.

Understandably, the area of influence of any one CIDG group was limited, and like the French outposts, the NLF found them relatively easy to bypass. If we accept the ratio of ten conventional forces to one guerrilla to be effective, the Strikers were outnumbered. Under these circumstances the existence of a degree of influence, no matter how limited, is a tribute to the Strikers and their teachers.

Even if the idea of guerrillas against guerrillas had been tested, there is still a contradiction: it is a reasonable assumption that if guerrillas depend for their existence as well as their success on the support of the people, two opposing guerrilla forces cannot have the support of the same people, and eventually, the propagandists and their bosses will know which of the two has the support. Perhaps this is why the idea was never implemented, or perhaps someone finally realized that no proof existed that Special Forces as an organization could conduct guerrilla warfare successfully as set forth in training doctrine. Those released from Special Forces to train people for the Bay of Pigs caper found a basic flaw in one of the axioms: What happened to the masses of people maltreated by the communists who would rush to the beaches as soon as they knew freedom was on the way?

Soldiers can train to work with indigenous peoples in other countries only by living with those peoples after proper preparation. Special Forces' past record in this department was excellent. Unlike other American GIs the Tenth Group in Bavaria were received in German homes, and mingled freely with the local inhabitants in their *Gasthäuser* and at their *Feste*. During war games the citizens sheltered and fed many of the teams, joined them in the field, acted as guides in the mountains, and passed on information about the "enemy." There was a real friendship between the people and these "different" soldiers; that a large number spoke German and an unusual percentage were European-born may have counted as much toward acceptance as their penchant for dressing like the locals.

Only the future could tell whether or not this type of rapport could be established with the Vietnamese—a people with a different color, culture, and an unknown language.

THIS IS AS GOOD A PLACE as any to dispense with the question of prejudice and discrimination in the Armed Forces. There have been civil laws against segregation, prejudice, and discrimination for many years, and ostensibly we fought a bloody war over the subject, but nobody contends that they have been eliminated. The armed forces, one of the first large segments of society to prohibit segregation, prejudice, and discrimination, have made greater strides in this field than the rest of society, yet many black GIs still feel there are two manuals of courts-martial.

Largely for economic reasons, in many areas of the country a large percentage of draftees and enlistees are Negro. Young men of draft age in higher income brackets have student deferments, while Negroes, out of school at an early age and with color against them, see the military as offering the lesser of two evils. Because they lack education or possibly have a police record many Negroes are turned away, but since by law the Army must accept a certain number of "sub-standard" personnel, a significant number make it. At the end of his two or three years of service, if he has been a reasonably good soldier, a Negro will have a corporal's (E-4) rating or perhaps be a sergeant, and while his white buddies eagerly await their return home, for him this is not necessarily a day of joy. The result is reenlistment, even though he might not like army life any more than his white counterpart.

As in our government, the basic criteria for promotion are time in grade and years of service. Since such a large percentage of eligible Negroes as compared to whites reenlist, there are many Negro senior NCOs—an encouragement to the younger men. But the Army has small cause for self-congratulation on its role in the War on Poverty. That so many of its citizens see the chances for equality as better in the most undemocratic of institutions is actually an indictment of that part of American society from which 80 percent of the military is drawn, bringing society's prejudices with them.

In 1955 I was one of four trainees refused service in a Manhattan, Kansas, restaurant because one of us was a Negro. The Army hadn't made the rule, but it hadn't put the restaurant off limits, either, even though many local merchants depended for their existence on the soldiers at Fort Riley.

Soldiers in Germany who worked side by side all day went to segregated bars at night. The bars were segregated not by the Germans but by the Americans—created in Germany by the same people who create black ghettos in America and in the same way. A few Negroes move in, the whites move out, and soon only Negroes are left. I saw this in Munich, Nürnberg, and Erlangen. Most of these bars were frequented by large numbers of "good-time girls" or prostitutes, and they were one of the more irrational reasons for the whites' moving on. Whites would have nothing to do with girls who slept with a Negro, and if a white soldier inadvertently shacked with a girl known to have had affairs with Negroes, he was held up to ridicule. This phenomenon is not restricted to

Germany—it is true in Japan, Korea, Viet-Nam, or wherever the U.S. Army goes; yet judging by the number of light-skinned Negroes in our country, repugnance and inhibitions don't carry over to tumbling in the sheets with a Negro girl.

When I reported to Fort Hood, Texas, in 1957, the Sergeant Major, who knew I was house hunting, handed me a map with the assurance that any area in the town of Killeen was safe, because niggers weren't allowed to live within the city limits. Killeen is another of those towns that depend on the military for their economic life; moreover, most of its citizens are either in or working for the Armed Services.

You may recall that it was the enlightened State of Texas that informed the Second Armored Division, prior to their return from Germany, of the jail sentences awaiting Negroes who had white wives. Most of these soldiers and their families were sent to places like Fort Dix, New Jersey, Fort Lewis, Washington, and Fort Ord, California. Negro soldiers with Negro families unable to get post housing moved up on the hill outside the Killeen city limits.

Officially, there is no prejudice in the Armed Forces, but officials with deep prejudices are placed all too often in positions of responsibility, as much in Special Forces as the rest of the Army.* There were Negroes in Special

* In 1961, prior to the huge buildup, Special Forces was composed of professional soldiers, a disproportionate share of whom come from the South, perhaps for the same economic reasons as the black soldier or because so many military posts are in the South. A large number of professionals originally from the North, after continual contact with Southerners and years of duty in the South become more "Rebel," with all the prejudices, than native Southerners. Prejudices are not left at the induction center, and often they are actually increased in service. The society which allowed

Forces in 1961, but the number was far below the average for the rest of the Army. In all fairness, however, Negroes were accepted by their white counterparts far better than in many other Army organizations.

Let me illustrate the point of prejudiced people in responsible positions. An officer responsible for many personnel appointments in Viet-Nam was irritated because the men he selected for the field teams of Project Delta were vetoed in favor of those selected by an NCO of lesser rank within the project. The official's choices were turned down not because the men were unqualified, but because each man had to be known to and recommended by two project members. One day, when the long list of rejections had become embarrassing, still another name was put forward. Only one man on the project knew him and only slightly. The personnel official gave the man a glowing report, extolling his fantastic ability in the field and passing along the commendations of well-known people with whom the man had worked. He was finally accepted on the understanding that if he was later considered unsuitable, he would be sent back to his original team. He turned out to be a real asset to the project—he worked well with American and Vietnamese soldiers, and his field ability was greater than some of the old-timers'. One night some time later Manny and I were invited for drinks at the official's villa. In the midst of a discussion about the project's last mission, our host interrupted and said, "One of the things I like most about Delta's field teams is that there aren't any niggers."

Manny's chair stopped rocking and he looked at me blankly.

the white man to live apart no longer shields him, and for the first time he has to take orders from a Negro—which he deeply resents.

My response was an incredulous, "What?"

"No niggers on the field teams. It's not that I'm prejudiced, you understand, but they don't have that extra something. You've done the right thing keeping them out of it."

"But it's not true," said Manny. "There is a Negro with us."

"Who?"

"Sergeant Handley—the man you recommended and sent. I've never turned down a man because of his color —only for the reasons I've always told you."

"He can't be. I've known him for years—he's white."

"Maybe his skin is, but not according to his record or what he says."

"You mean you knew it when you accepted him?" Our host was really disturbed.

"That's right."

The official slumped back in his chair, shaking his head. "I just can't believe it. If I had known that, I would never have recommended him." He suddenly leaned forward. "Come on, Manny. You're just pulling my leg, aren't you?"

●　　●　　●

The prejudice is there, perhaps hidden a little better but present nevertheless, a dangerous trait for people who are supposed to work with indigenous peoples.

It has been officially denied that there is any "anti-Negro bias" (*i.e.*, prejudice) in Special Forces. It never occurred to me that such a thing would officially be admitted since officially it doesn't exist—it's printed in the regulations to prove it. Officially, we are not a racist nation.

Donald Duncan

In Viet-Nam there was an ironic twist. Initially, Special Forces worked almost exclusively with the Montagnards, people barely tolerated by the ethnic Vietnamese, who not only think of them as animals but have treated them as such for years. Strangely enough, most of the men in Special Forces not only got along well with the dark-skinned "yards" but genuinely liked them, and even though the Americans were quartered apart from them, the mountain people returned the friendship. The men of the "A" teams saved their dislike for the Vietnamese and were openly contemptuous of their indigenous counterparts, though some had a "my Vietnamese" who was stoutly defended as "different" from the others. The regime the "A" teams were helping was held in such low esteem that it often seemed they were in secret league against it, and when various tribes would rebel against the government, there was no doubt as to which side had the sympathy, if not on the official level, certainly on the working level. General Khan virtually accused Special Forces of instigating the 1964 rebellion. Nobody thought it strange to hear these soldiers railing against the Saigon government and the Vietnamese for their stupidity and ignorance because of the injustices perpetrated against the impoverished minority group, "who, after all, were born and raised in Viet-Nam, too."

Contact with the Vietnamese, from which the insurgents drew their major strength and whose hearts and minds had to be won, was restricted by the Americans to the essential minimum. Other than their counterparts and officials with whom they reluctantly did business, the only Vietnamese the Americans had contact with were the taxi drivers and the bar-girls.

EVENTUALLY I became involved with another quota. Buttons were pressed, a computer buzzed, hummed, and dropped my "DO NOT BEND, FOLD, SPINDLE, OR MUTILATE" into the slot—and I was on my way to Viet-Nam.

•　•　•

I wiped the condensation from one of the military jet's few windows. To my right was the blue-green ocean; below and as far to the left as I could see stretched a flat area divided into brown and green patches; dark lines of trees marked the courses of meandering rivers along which miniature villages clustered. The change of pressure in my ears marked our descent, and I felt the familiar excitement of arriving at a new place to start a new job.

As we circled the city I was impressed by its size. From the detachment of our pressurized plane the rows of tile roofs, the miniature cars on the arterials, the scaled-down streets made Saigon seem little different from a hundred other cities seen from the air, just as the countryside could have been farmland anywhere.

After the dim coolness in the jet the glare was blinding and the heat of the sun and blacktop staggering. Sergeant Vanouker and I slipped away from the MAAG and MACV * assignees and sought the coolness of a terminal building to phone for transportation to Special Forces. A water cooler bore a sign warning against using the water to fill canteens.

The thirty-minute ride from Tan Son Nhut into town convinced us that this was not "just another city." Impossible to take in all at once, it was confused movement, masses of people, mind-deafening noise, smells drawn out by the appalling heat and humidity. Hundreds of blue and white Renault taxis, horns blowing, darted around roofed carts pulled by tiny horses. Red-tired bicycles wove past potholes, pedestrians, and other cyclists with complete disregard for traffic from cross streets. Young men on beeping scooters competed with honking taxis, while dainty girls miraculously maintained side-saddle positions on the back. Sirens screaming, motorcycles cleared a path at an intersection for a speeding official in a black limousine.

Smells: exhaust fumes from the endless numbers of taxis and military vehicles; human excrement; the foul, stagnant black mud and water of the world's dirtiest river passing under Cong Ly Street; fish guts rotting in the garbage piled on a streetcorner; everywhere the pungency of *nuoc-mam*.

People—continuous masses of them: toddlers, barefoot and dirty-faced, wearing only shirts that never quite reached the navels of their protruding bellies, watching our progress with large solemn eyes; older children staring unblinkingly, barefoot, wearing overall-type trousers with the crotch seam opened—a practical alteration elim-

* Military Aid and Advisory Group; Military Assistance Command, Viet-Nam.

inating the need for diapers; schoolgirls in blue butterfly sunhats waiting for us to pass, while young boys in white shirts stretched out their hands, chanting "Okay—Salem," thus exhausting their English vocabulary; delicate young women in varicolored *ao-dais*, wearing conical sunhats or carrying parasols, floating gracefully through the throngs; slim hipless men in white shirts and severely tailored black trousers walking hand in hand—a custom misunderstood by us as by most newcomers; straggly-bearded old men in wide-legged pajama trousers, their stooped shoulders covered with loose-fitting jackets, ignoring our passing; crones clopping and jogging, square water cans suspended from poles bent over their narrow shoulders, also wearing full trousers but with flared shirt-waists buttoned tight against wasted breasts (an old woman spat a stream of pink juice in our path—habit or gesture—revealing a mouthful of black teeth). Except for the smallest children the people all looked remarkably clean—an incredible accomplishment in the heat, dirt, and squalor.

Houses sided on open bicycle shops, machine shops, furniture shops, herb shops, barber shops whose signs depicted marcelled men and the words нос тос, and shops offering gold teeth caps in various styles; every fifth shop displayed Western-style clothing or shoes. Bars were ubiquitous, most with American names and faced with grenade-proof screening. Hole-in-the-wall houses made from packing cases and holding three or four families sat next to spacious villas protected by military guards.

Our driver added his horn to the din and pushed through, narrowly avoiding disaster at every corner. At a Caltex station we noticed hundreds of tiny horseshoes left behind in the soft asphalt when their owners had trotted obediently to market. Two blocks past a traffic circle where a thousand vehicles were playing chicken, we outbluffed the traffic on Le Van Duyet Street and turned into a gate guarded by Vietnamese soldiers— Camp Goodman, headquarters for the III Corps Tactical Zone "B" Detachment of Special Forces.

During the three days it took Vanouker and me to get to Special Forces Headquarters in Nha Trang, we gained an impression of life in Saigon that would be intensified in the future. From the men at the "B" Detachment we received directions to the downtown area and a card with a small map and our address in English and Vietnamese; they advised us on the best rates for changing money on the black market and how much to pay for a taxi. Tu Do, lower Hai Ba Trung, and Nguyen Hue were recommended areas to visit.

Whatever it was we had expected when we walked the length of Tu Do, from John F. Kennedy Square to the waterfront, we certainly weren't prepared for what we found. The street was ablaze with a garish hodgepodge of colored neon signs. Music and crowds of Americans weaving boisterously to the next bar spilled into the street. The restaurants and clothing stores catered to American trade, and the Indian bookstore was doing a brisk business changing GI greenbacks into piastres. Streetcorners were crowded with competing cycles and little kiosks where a *mama-san* sold American cigarettes, dirty pictures, lottery tickets, and condoms foil-wrapped to look like five-dollar gold pieces. Small boys grabbed at us: "You want change money . . . You give me ten 'p' . . . Cherry girl very cheap . . . Shine shoes . . . My sister number-one fuckie, you like . . ."

In the Pavillon Bar we had our first experience (but by no means our last) buying "whickey-Coke" for a hostess and playing the bar-girls' version of gin rummy.

After three or four others we tried a larger establishment advertising air conditioning—it was jammed and hot in spite of the cooling system, and sweating bodies struggled desperately on a miniature dance floor to the deafening accompaniment of electric guitars. It was here that we received our first Vietnamese evaluation of Special Forces, which by now regarded itself as America's military Peace Corps.

As soon as we sat down two girls joined us, and rather than argue with our uninvited guests, we ordered drinks all around. After assuring us they were "number one" and "me no butterfly," one asked where we worked. Vanouker gave her the card with the Special Forces address and she squinted in the dim light to read it.

"Ohhh!" she squealed, smiling approval. "You Special Forces . . . Special Forces number one. They eat pussy!"

I lost half my drink in my lap and the other half through my nose; Vanouker knocked his over grabbing for the card and tried to draw his burning ears into his shoulders. The GIs at the next table found it hilarious. A couple of hours later, when Vanouker caught me saying, "What's a nice girl like you doing in a . . ." he insisted we leave.

Nha Trang, supposedly my permanent base, was only a processing point. Three days after I arrived the Operations and Intelligence sections, the Special Forces commander, and I moved to Saigon, because in-fighting was apparently not restricted to the shores of the United States. Certain regulars at MACV and MAAG Headquarters in Saigon were saying unfavorable things about Special Forces in an attempt to wrest control of their operations away from them, and their funds, supplies, and publicity. In addition, Colonel Lam Son, Commander of the Vietnamese Special Forces (LLDB), was forsaking the comforts of his palatial seaside villa in Nha Trang to spend more and more time in Saigon, the better to keep up with the impending coups, petits coups, and other political machinations. To protect Special Forces and defend himself against both elements, the colonel asked for and received permission to move to Saigon.

Before returning to the "Pearl of the Orient," I drew my field equipment, a new Colt Armelite AR-15, and eighty rounds of ammunition. Unlike stateside, the weapon and the ammo were kept in the barracks—until now there had been little to suggest that this was a combat zone.

●   ●   ●

Life in Saigon and my job in the headquarters as an Area Specialist Sergeant for III and IV Corps Tactical Zone weren't exactly what I'd had in mind when I came to Viet-Nam. At Nha Trang, I had been surprised by house-girls making beds and shining boots, a mess hall overrun with Vietnamese KPs and cooks, hundreds of laborers policing the area, watering flowers, and loading planes. In Saigon, where all the NCOs lived in an air-conditioned hotel with maid service and a seemingly inexhaustible supply of girls from the bar across the street, the greatest hardship was trying to get to sleep. Most didn't even try after the bar closed—then the bar-girls flowed in, clacking wooden heels on the corridor tiles and shrieking; men shouted and laughed, bells rang and showers ran.

My assignment as an Area Specialist, which I had resented, turned out to be fortunate, eventually leading to my becoming part of Project Delta. Primarily I had to be as completely informed as possible on what was happening at Special Forces camps in the two corps areas comprising the southern half of what was known as South Viet-Nam. This involved keeping statistics on file, and keeping operations and intelligence maps up to date; each morning the colonel was briefed on the past twenty-four hours' activities, based on daily situation reports from the various camps. Ample time was left for traveling to all the camps, necessary in order to know what was going on; this gave me the opportunity of seeing more than most of the men assigned to "A" teams who are often isolated in camps for six months. Before leaving Viet-Nam, I spent time in towns, villages, and hamlets, in camps, and in cities from Hue to Ha Tien, and I was involved in combat operations in every type of terrain the country had to offer.

Working in a headquarters also gave me the advantage of getting the "big picture," of finding out how and why certain decisions are made, of gaining a feeling for political maneuvering. I was surprised to see how many reports were passed back and forth marked "NOFORN," * which meant that the lowest ranking American clerk but no Vietnamese under any circumstances, regardless of rank, could see them. Many were evaluations of the Vietnamese military or officials, and differed from the glowing tributes paid ARVN in the official American press releases. The LLDB had a variation of musical chairs. When a camp commander was caught stealing too much money meant for the Strike Forces, or selling too much military equipment to the black market, or showing cowardice once too often, the pressure would be put on to have him relieved. He would be transferred to another

* No Foreign Dissemination—*i.e.*, not to be shown to Vietnamese personnel, official or otherwise.

camp whose commander was transferred to another and so on. The variation was to promote the offender and send him to headquarters.

•   •   •

Having arrived in Viet-Nam well motivated and wanting to help "preserve freedom and democracy and aid our Vietnamese friends," I was completely taken aback by my contemporaries' attitude toward our "friends." In the office, the hotel, the bars and the camps I heard constant variations on the contempt theme in very colorful language: the government was rotten, the officials corrupt, ARVN cowardly, the LLDB all three, the man-in-the-street an ignorant thief, and all the women whores.

The part about women is interesting. Prior to my arrival and for some time after, Special Forces teams drew a nine-to-sixteen-dollar per diem beyond their other pay and allowances during their six-month tour in Viet-Nam. It was not uncommon on forays into town for a man to spend twenty dollars in a bar, of which the girl received half, and then to pay another ten to buy the girl out and take her to an air-conditioned hotel. Depending on the time of the month, this could amount to thirty-nine hundred piastres—in a country where a stevedore earned seventy piastres a day and had to buy on a market inflated by GI money. Little wonder that more and more girls became prostitutes. Having obtained what they wanted with their money, the soldiers then condemned the girls. For those stationed in town the thing to do was to obtain a permanent "shack," which eliminated sitting in a bar every night. The savings were passed along to the girl in cash or in rent, and the GI further supplemented her income by purchasing hair spray, cigarettes, liquor, and transistor radios, which she sold for great profit on the black market.

The girls' enthusiasm in their work and the GIs' opinion of the Vietnamese females as lovers seemed to be based on mutual contempt—most GIs described love-making with a Vietnamese as a higher form of masturbation; the remainder argued that it was not.

Many of these girls must have been in the NLF's employ on some basis, but if not, someone was missing a good bet, because the amount of military information passed around these bars was incredible. Pilots talked about future operations in front of a hostess, under the impression that because she spoke poor English and was dumb (synonymous with Vietnamese), she wouldn't understand. In a Vung Tau bar I caught a hostess off guard and found that her English compared quite favorably with, and in some instances was better than, that of many of the GIs buying her drinks. Asked why she used "bar-girl" English ("You be ni'me . . . You no go my *hau*"), she said it was expected of her and she made more money that way; later I learned that she was a third-year law student, which put her academically far ahead of most of her clientele.

After a while it wasn't difficult to understand why Americans generally held to their low opinion of the Vietnamese. Their contact was generally restricted to Vietnamese military and civilian officials, bar-girls, speculators, most of whom were all the things said about them, and for good reason—they had excellent teachers: the Americans. A U.S. agency competing with another for services, material, or machinery, would pay bribes to get the job done, and then call the recipient a crook; from bribes it was only one step to kickbacks. Beer and liquor, unattainable in the PX in August 1965, could be purchased, with PX stickers attached, in any bar downtown. Who was the source? After dependents were shipped home and there was only a handful of nurses in Nha Trang, case after case of hair spray was sold every month (often, a sign would appear, saying, "ONE CAN PER CUSTOMER—SHE'LL HAVE TO WAIT, MEN"), and there were some other strange bestsellers in an all-male market— Kotex, nail polish, cologne, cosmetics; liquor and transistor radios were also big movers, as were Salem cigarettes, the Vietnamese favorite.

With a bar-girl's income higher than the Premier's official salary, it made good sense for an official to be in on the take. With most of the officials being paid off, there was little reason for the Vietnamese people to respect them. When most military officers were using their positions to enhance their personal wealth, there was good cause for low morale among the troops. When the majority of the Vietnamese looked upon these people with contempt, it was not surprising that the Americans did, too. We shouldn't assume that most Vietnamese aren't aware of what and who has caused the mess or wonder why Americans are seldom invited into Vietnamese homes.

●　　●　　●

As the year passed, it became apparent that for all purposes the war was over—what little fighting there was, was usually around a Special Forces camp. ARVN usually announced plans for a large operation far enough in advance to insure no contact when launched, and on those rare occasions when reportable action occurred, it seemed to be an accident or the result of American initiative. I became expert at padding field reports to give the impression at briefings that things were really happening. For the specialist in I Corps Area (Da Nang, Hue) it was really tough because of the lack of action, and to invent something was almost impossible.

According to the intelligence map, the area controlled by Saigon was almost non-existent. Roads were still open in many places but only with the permission of the NLF, which collected tolls from government traffic.* No matter how large an army they took, ARVN couldn't venture into many areas. So well did the NLF control some areas that they held elections, built and ran schools and hospitals, had their own markets, collected taxes, and repaired roads and bridges. Instances of NLF companies surrounding entire ARVN battalions were becoming embarrassingly frequent. In such cases the Saigon forces were often allowed to leave, after discarding their weapons and deserting their American advisors.† It was apparent that more Vietnamese in the countryside, at all levels, were making accommodations with the NLF. Agent reports frequently told of unarmed NLF information teams entering villages next to government posts, putting on a skit, and staying the night.

The more this went on, the more desperately the U.S. military tried to get things going. Pressure was put on the "A" teams to make more and longer patrols with their Strike Forces, and the Saigon "B" team commander

* When it was no longer profitable or convenient, the roads were closed. None of the roads were opened until well after September 1965—by the U.S. troops. After 1964 rail traffic halted.

† If this seems inconsiderate, it should be remembered that many times when ARVN did stand and fight on the advice of their advisors, and things got rough, U.S. helicopters would come in and pick up the Americans, leaving the troops to fight alone.

was personally directing field operations in an effort to run down the enemy and force a fight. As more and more areas fell under NLF control, the number of "free bomb zones" increased; U.S. pilots went hunting, trying to draw fire. New definitions of a Viet Cong came into vogue: any gook running from an aircraft; any dead Vietnamese.

Unfavorable field reports, couched in language intended to throw the best possible light on the action, were rewritten and consolidated in the intermediate headquarters to make them more graphic. The end result, implying "see-how-well-we-do-with-the-little-we've-got," was a not too subtle plea for more *U.S.* troops and equipment.

In late 1964 or early 1965 anyone who had suggested that there still would be nothing settled in 1966, despite complete control, four hundred thousand troops, and SAC and TAC dropping five tons of bombs for every square mile of Viet-Nam, and that responsible officials would be saying two million troops and five more years, would have been marched off to a couch captain.

•   •   •

As the frustrations inherent in fighting a paper war increased, so did the frequency of "It's a lousy war, but it's the only one we've got," usually followed by "If only we had American troops and full American control, we could clean this up in no time." The general attitude seemed to be that the Vietnamese were too stupid to know what was good for them and incapable of appreciating or understanding the democracy our military had brought to them.

Perhaps the "It's a lousy war but . . ." should be explained. First of all, with only a few exceptions the American soldiers in Viet-Nam in 1964 were professionals, and among professionals there is always some cynicism when dealing with a civilian populace, even more with a foreign populace. They chafed at the "ridiculous" restrictions imposed on them by politicians—the "advisory" concept never was popular and life was a continual game to circumvent it. Officers and NCOs alike itched to be able to give orders instead of advice—which was more often than not ignored—and frustration grew at the inability to locate the enemy or identify him: How do you tell the enemy from the people? In spite of the $1.5 million being spent daily, and the cajoling, pleading, and browbeating, the political and military situations were deteriorating. But there were compensations, and there were reasons why the military wanted to stimulate things and why the reports and briefings reaching the American public tried to be encouraging.

To military men there is nothing worse than not having a war—not that they're anxious to be killed, but as a means of justifying their existence. With a war or the immediate threat of one, the military gains in prestige and other rewards. If it's a war where the risks are small, so much the better. In 1964 there were fifteen thousand "advisors" in Viet-Nam, twelve to thirteen thousand in Saigon—a new bureaucratic high even for the U.S. military. A soldier flying to a countryside post as little as four days a month could draw per diem, collect combat pay, and log hours toward an Air Medal; if shot at, or if he could find someone to sign a certificate saying he had been, he could earn a Combat Infantryman's Badge—then back to the gin and tonic. Prior to Viet-Nam, those with less than ten years of service had never seen combat, hence had had no opportunities for medals. An officer's chances for future promotion are enhanced by troop-leading experience in combat. After it was announced that all medals normally granted only in wartime could be won in Viet-Nam, the number of volunteers for duty there increased.

Viet-Nam not only gave the military an opportunity to increase its bureaucracy, it also offered a means of gaining a direct voice in U.S. policy. As the prime gatherer of information on the "Vietnamese situation," the military's interpretation is based on military values, judging the appropriateness of information and passing along military recommendations. The men responsible withhold information not because they are dishonest or disloyal but because they believe it is in the interests of military security or sincerely feel that civilians just wouldn't understand or appreciate the danger to our country. To the military mind this behavior is not only honest, it is loyal to country and a rational thing to do. But it is on this information that national policy is based and public opinion formed.

The impression grew that only if they could find a "nice" war elsewhere would the military ever recommend getting out of Viet-Nam, but meanwhile they were determined to make do with the one they had. Various schemes for hanging on through 1964 were proposed and rejected. General Harkins was replaced by General Westmoreland in April, and General Taylor was appointed American Ambassador to South Viet-Nam. Under U.S. sponsorship teams were trained to infiltrate Laos (Project Delta) *

* Infiltrating Laos posed no particular problems since teams could parachute in, be taken in by helicopter, or walk in. The decision to drop the troops in (despite increased danger of compromise, and greater expense, and a complicated procedure) was based on a distrust of the Vietnamese soldiers. Without American leaders, it was concluded, the Vietnamese would make only a nominal penetration by land, wait a decent period, and return with phony reports.

and North Viet-Nam (Special Operations Group—SAG). The more ambitious projects had to be shelved until after the elections, but military preparations were made (such as the Cam Ranh Bay project) and the American people prepared. The word "insurgency" was used less often as the year progressed—all the experts and their plans to defeat the guerrillas couldn't be wrong. Since our concept of insurgency had to be correct, the enemy must be cheating.

With the guerrillas continuing to gain the initiative, it became harder to keep up a favorable kill ratio by exaggerating the number of enemy casualties, so the American people were to be informed that we were fighting invaders—alarms were sounded and everybody bent to the task of finding something that could be construed as proof of the allegation, despite the inherent dangers. "Invasion," as normally applied to war, would mean that Viet-Nam had been attacked by a foreign state—which made "fighting invaders" somewhat awkward, since the foreigners fighting in Viet-Nam were U.S. troops.*

The American people had to be convinced that the communists had violated the Geneva Agreements of 1954—which wasn't too difficult, since we all know communists never keep agreements—but in other parts of the world it wasn't quite so simple because three of the more important parts of the agreements stated:

1. Neither zone would make international alliances or receive military help from the outside. (Before the

tions was making sure we did not drop any of the teams on or near any of the CIA teams, called Hardnose, already in Laos.)

* Nobody, least of all the Vietnamese, denies the difference in accent, speech, and other minor things between a native of Hanoi and a native of Ca Mau; they are probably less foreign to each other, however, than a Bostonian and an Atlantan.

ink was dry, MAAG took over the training of the Saigon Army and SEATO came into being complete with its protocol for Viet-Nam.)

2. Elections were to be held in July 1956 to assure the unification of the two zones (not countries). (Under our advisement Ngo Dinh Diem refused to prepare the elections because the predicted results would not be favorable to him and the "free world.")

3. The administrative separation of the two zones was provisional, "And should not in any way be interpreted as constituting a political or territorial boundary" (Article I, Paragraph 6 of the Final Declaration).

In 1964, nine years after the zones were to have been united, and in the absence of any proof of the presence of any Hanoi troops in the southern zone, the world witnessed a foreign power in Viet-Nam, the United States, accusing Vietnamese of invading Viet-Nam. By the end of 1965 the American people were convinced and we had a hundred thousand troops in the southern zone, resulting in PAVN troops' going south in an attempt to throw them out. The prophecy had become self-fulfilling—once again the facts agreed with the propaganda.

In January 1964, prior to my arrival, there had been a near coup and a coup—the first when General Duong Van Minh ousted the last civilian control from the Saigon government, the second when General Nguyen Khanh ousted Minh fourteen days later. Shortly thereafter, the NLF took over Tay Ninh province except for the provincial capital. In March a law was passed virtually eliminating free speech and freedom of the press; talk of negotiations, neutrality, peace were punishable offenses. Corruption increased and political maneuvering for power was rampant. Conscription procedures could barely keep up with desertions from the Army. It was a can of worms, and people talked not about helping "the government" or "the people," but about fighting communism and saving the Vietnamese from and in spite of themselves.

Situations had to be shown in the best light to back up past propaganda. Since the formation of a stable government is impossible in the midst of a conflict, political turmoil was blamed on the NLF, even though during impending and actual coups, NLF-initiated actions actually decreased. Even while the sentiment among the U.S. forces in Viet-Nam was "There aren't ten slopes worth even one GI," the American people were soon to be asked to die all over Viet-Nam for anti-communism.

The relative value of American and Vietnamese life after we took control is exemplified by the willingness to destroy a whole village rather than risk losing one GI. Nonetheless, official releases spoke of our gallant Vietnamese friends struggling heroically against the communist aggressors. The U.S. military's true estimation of ARVN as an effective fighting force can be judged by the decision in 1966 to remove all Vietnamese troops from combat situations and use them in rear-echelon "pacification" programs. This allowed us to get rid of a liability without losing face and provided for complete American control of all military action.*

●　　●　　●

It might be interesting to quote from official documents, dated from 1964 to early 1965, not released for public consumption. Most of these carry the warning:

* The Vietnamese can be ferocious fighters, but a soldier is only as good as his training, leadership, and motivation—sadly lacking in ARVN—and without any one, the other two are of little value.

"Under no circumstances whatsoever is this information to be released or shown to Vietnamese officials."

> . . . the sympathetic support of a large segment of the population also helps the insurgents. The insurgents openly recruit in the province and have little trouble securing the local forces necessary to provide information and shelter to passing units . . .

On the replacement of village chiefs by Saigon:

> . . . the residents cling to their former hamlet way of life and seem to resent the intruders who have come to set up the administrative machinery necessary . . .

On civic action:

> . . . the social revolution associated with pacification may be failing to take hold for lack of a firm base of people willing to support and defend their government.

On voluntary militia:

> . . . without an ID card a person is a virtual prisoner in his house; he cannot leave the hamlet for fear of being caught without it and accused of being a Viet Cong. Thus, if true, the threat of losing their ID card was the greater of the two evils confronting the men, and they readily joined the militia.

On propaganda:

> . . . The information program is one of the glaring failures of the pacification program . . . the *Chieu Hoi* [Open Arms—a program to entice the insurgents back to the government] program has been an even worse failure. There have been only three returnees to the village in the past three years.

Are those opposed to the Saigon regime communists?

> . . . that many of the people in the area fought with the Viet Minh against the French and are proud of it, does not necessarily mean they are communist or even sympathizers.

The remarks of an appointed village chief:

> . . . Seventy percent of the village population are Viet Cong sympathizers; perhaps one percent openly support the government; the rest are indifferent.

Are the Viet Cong of the RVN the Viet Minh of the DVN?

> The NLF have skillfully assumed the pose of the Viet Minh.

Co-operation and trust of the Saigon regime:

> . . . the people will do what we force them to do . . . they have not seen any government people who have been truthful to them.

There was, in one document, a poem translated by its author with the following comment:

> . . . a poem appeared in a central Viet-Nam newspaper and was immediately attacked in several Saigon dailies as being communist-inspired and detrimental . . . It is reproduced here . . . to express what many of the Vietnamese . . . feel and think but fear to admit openly . . .

The Last Act

The corpses lie in disorder,
Their faces cannot be seen.
They do not have any clothing,
Lying together on a piece of land,
Poor, starving and miserable.

The old mother leaning on a cane,
Tears running down in two rows,
"Sir, are these communists?"
"Sir, are these nationalists?"
Sobbing, mother bends her head to see,
"No, these are Vietnamese."
Living together in the same village,
Children of the same mother,
That black hair and red blood
Of this pug-nosed yellow skin.
Here are the rifles and bullets of foreigners.
Outside, the garden has been burned
And the children dig potatoes
Like hungry dogs,
Seeing a dim future.
The vultures come.
Animals and human beings,
Neither can recognize the other.

The same individual also reported this:

Perhaps the answer for Vietnam is not Western-style democracy but what was recently suggested by a Vietnamese: "The only way to save our country is with a basic change . . . a new policy . . . humanitarian socialism . . ." The requirement for a successful government system in Vietnam, one that is born out of Vietnamese considerations, it does indicate that the idea of *nhon dao* [humanity or to be humane; the main characteristic the people would like in their government] is held by more than just the Vietnamese peasants.

He was quoting from a statement made in *Newsweek* (October 19, 1964) by Colonel Pham Ngoc, the man who tried to get rid of General Khanh in February 1965. For putting this heretical blasphemy in an official document, I hope he met a better fate than the colonel.

THE CONTENTION that we are becoming a total military state will be loudly denied, and those protesting the loudest will be the legions themselves—the three million dressed in the blue and green of our armed legions and those in the flannel suits and narrow-brimmed hats.*

So pervasive is the propensity to think in military terms that America's everyday language has become one large euphemism. The prospect for war is not cause for sober reflection because the word which once meant the stink of mangled bodies on a battlefield and man's inhumanity to man is now a synonym for security, determination, sincerity, and betterment. And so we accept "War on Poverty," "War on Crime," "War on Air Pollution," and the classic of our time, "Peace Offensive." "Peace" to many now means a cessation of armed conflict which enables our enemies to gain strength.

George Orwell points out that we use this type of speech in

> . . . the defense of the indefensible; actions which can only be defended . . . by arguments which are too brutal for most people to face and which do not square with the professed aims of political parties.

* The narrowing of hatbrims seems to have kept pace with the ever narrowing definition of reality; note the brimless Green Beret.

Although he died before our total involvement in Viet-Nam, one example he offered applies directly to the American rationale for our actions there:

Defenseless villages are bombarded from the air, the inhabitants driven out into the countryside, the cattle machinegunned, the huts set on fire with incendiary bullets: this is called *pacification*.*

Those who oppose our actions in Viet-Nam seem at a loss to understand not only why we are there, but why so many people in and out of government support it. To the military, our involvement is perfectly rational; and if the danger as defined by the military is accepted as accurate the whole thing does make sense. A nation conditioned to think in military terms, we have accepted the definition; therefore a majority feel our position is just.

The American people know that the politically unsophisticated Vietnamese might opt for a socialist state (substitute "communism"; equates with EVIL) if they had that choice. But since that would threaten the United States, we cannot allow it to happen, and therefore it is only right that all necessary steps be taken to prevent such a thing, even if it is temporarily rough on the Vietnamese. The program, however, has to be acceptable to people who take pride in their children, swimming pools, and schools. Orwell shows how this is done:

While freely conceding that the [Saigon] government exhibits certain features which the humanitarian may be inclined to deplore, we must, I think, agree that a certain curtailment of the right to political opposition is an unavoidable concomitant of transitional periods, and that the rigors which the [Vietnamese] people have been called upon to undergo

* *A Collection of Essays by George Orwell* (New York: Doubleday, 1954). His italics.

have been amply justified in the sphere of concrete achievement.*

Orwell translates this as: "I believe in killing off your opponents when you can get good results by doing so."

•   •   •

Compare our own Revolutionary War to Viet-Nam. The American Revolutionists were not responsible for the conditions which led to armed conflict, although the leaders exploited them to motivate the citizenry; nor was Ho Chi Minh responsible for conditions in Viet-Nam. In both instances a colonial power was responsible, and the struggle was not simply to replace those at the top (reform) but to implement a concept of government tailored to meet the people's needs and to develop the country (revolution). Both borrowed from old laws in declaring the new—the United States from England, Viet-Nam from France. (Viet-Nam's Declaration of Independence uses passages from the American Declaration of Independence and the French Declaration of the Rights of Man and Citizen.) All leaders were not motivated purely by altruism or patriotism. Only after recourse to political action had been exhausted and there had been various forms of repression did armed conflict begin. In the initial stages neither was strong enough to confront the opposing forces, so they resorted to sabotage and guerrilla warfare (the American version was less sophisticated). Americans not agreeing with the Revolutionists were considered traitors and sanctions were taken against them; the same is true in Viet-Nam. There

* *Ibid.* "Saigon" and "Vietnamese" have been substituted for "Soviet" and "Russian."

is another similarity, one that Americans tend to forget: many major powers considered the American Revolution's political ideology a threat to world order; many nations besides England felt that the Revolution had to be crushed lest the concept spread and destroy the world or make it unfit to live in.

The two countries won their respective struggles, and there similarity ends. But let us assume that it didn't. Suppose that a powerful third nation had offered to intervene in the last stages of the American Revolution, threatening to annihilate both the country and the people (as in 1954, when the U.S. offered France nuclear bombs to defeat the Viet Minh). England, fearing the consequences, refuses the offer (as France did) and offers to negotiate in order to withdraw. Although they have won all but a few towns, and victory is in sight, the Americans agree to sit down rather than shed any more blood. At the British-American meeting it is decided that the only way to disengage the opposing armies so the English could withdraw would be to divide the country temporarily, so the Americans agree to bring their Southern armies north, even though it means the soldiers will have to leave their homes and families for two years. The English move their armies south and use New Orleans as an administrative capital while arranging the mechanics of withdrawal.

The third nation is now furious; using their power and money, they install an exiled American, opposed to the Revolutionists, as head of a *de facto* government in New Orleans. At the end of two years the English leave, but the third government is well entrenched; they help build an army and police force, which kills or jails anybody opposed to the New Orleans regime, and refuse to let the country reunite, insisting that the United States is actually two countries.

Had this happened, wouldn't the Americans in the South have fought and wouldn't those cooperating with the New Orleans regime—especially those mayors and governors appointed by New Orleans—have received short shrift? Northerners would surely have helped their fellow Americans in the South (although I am not sure we would have shown the same restraint in preventing the Southern troops from going home for ten years). Had the Americans come south, they would hardly have felt like aggressors or invaders. It seems fair to assume that the Americans, so blatantly betrayed, would be in no hurry to sit down and talk to this third nation, especially if one of the conditions was that only those in the North had a right to talk, and that the country was to remain separated and retain the politics of the foreigner.

After President Johnson conceded that the Viet Cong could have their views represented at negotiations which would otherwise exclude them, the Australian journalist Wilfred Burchett pointed out in a UPI dispatch (December 10, 1965), which said:

. . . Washington has made it clear to Premier Nguyen Cao Ky that it will firmly adhere to two fundamentals:
1. In any peace agreement, the National Liberatioin Front of the Viet Cong would be denied any status which could lead to the formation of a coalition government. 2. There could be nothing in any peace treaty which would hinder the South Vietnamese government in its program of total "pacification" of the countryside. This is considered necessary in order to deny the guerrillas any bases from which to make political inroads or a military comeback.

The United States has said for some time that it would not negotiate with the National Liberation

Front, the political arm of the Viet Cong. But at one time officials indicated that some of the non-communist elements fighting with the Viet Cong might be considered eligible for participation in the country's political life. This apparently has now been ruled out in the U.S. determination to prevent anything which might serve as the germ of a coalition government.

In short, if you're willing to let the South be the way WE want it, we can stop fighting. The dispatch is revealing for two other reasons: It refers to "non-communists fighting with the Viet Cong"; and it repeats an old myth about the Viet Cong.

"Viet Cong," a pejorative coined by Ngo Dinh Diem to describe those opposed to his regime, is supposed to mean "Vietnamese Communist," although when it was coined, communists constituted a minority of the opposition to Diem. The opposition banded together and formed a united political front known as the National Liberation Front. The NLF's military arm is the Liberation Army, and the NLF also directs the local militia, or if you prefer, part-time guerrillas (the Army are the full-time guerrillas). It is the NLF's military arm which we insist on calling "Viet Cong." Our propagandists would have us believe that a miscellaneous group of people met one day and said, "Let's have an insurrection just for hellery," and went out shooting. Actually, the shooting results from political decisions to achieve political ends and is controlled by politics, not the other way around.

●　　●　　●

I invite you to reread the dispatch.

V

"*The continual necessity for their services enhances the importance of the soldier, and proportionably degrades the condition of the citizen. The military state becomes elevated above the civil . . . and by degrees the people are brought to consider the soldiery not only as their protectors, but as their superiors.*"

ALEXANDER HAMILTON
The Federalist VIII

THE ADVENTURES in Part II were not included to titillate those who enjoy gory war stories. Any one of a dozen other such field trips could have served that purpose. But this particular story is especially significant to me personally as a result of the preceding trip into an NLF stronghold area.

On that trip my American partner and I found ourselves in what looked like a completely hopeless situation. We were on our way to rejoin our Vietnamese team after a private scouting foray, when, without warning, rifle fire broke out all around us. My partner was put out of action by one of the first rounds. I was alone, with no hope of assistance (the team was instructed to get out of the area in the event of trouble), with my back to a clearing and only a small shrub in front of me. I couldn't see my attackers and the only indication I had of their numbers was that they were expending ammo like tomorrow the war would be fought with bows and arrows. Having nothing to shoot at, I could only crouch behind my flimsy cover while bullets clipped away branches and scarred the sand an inch from my knee. It was not my first time under fire, so I experienced only the normal amount of fear. My adrenalin pumping, I assessed the situation, considered and rejected four courses of action—and the truth struck: I was going to die.

I don't mean I thought I would probably die; I mean I was going to die. No matter what I did, no matter how brilliantly I schemed, maneuvered, or fought, I was in a hopeless box. My most optimistic estimate of the time factor was twenty seconds, but at least one bullet seemed likely to find its way through the bush much sooner than that. In my line of work, facing the possibility or even the probability of death was not uncommon, but facing the certainty of death was unique.

The split second I accepted that stark reality a strange thing happened. I looked at my hand to see how I was reacting physically to my situation and discovered it wasn't me looking; rather it was—Me. I wasn't startled or surprised that Me had stepped out and was standing to the side, evaluating. I checked my weapon and held fire, waiting for a target; Me nodded approvingly. The inside of my mind was explored in detail and each fraction of my skin spoke to Me. Odd how that bullet that splashed the sand next to my leg didn't disturb that magnificently structured ant. I wonder why I never noticed how many fuzzy hairs are on each of these beautiful leaves. I felt it . . . the hair on my arms were friends smiling at me and my skin asked if it could fly . . . happiness. For the first time I was alive in the world—with death a second away. Life was beautiful. I wanted life. It had nothing to do with death. It wasn't that I didn't want to die—death was irrelevant—I wanted to live. I looked over at Me to pass on this beautiful fact and received a knowing smile.

●　　●　　●

I'll omit the details of a most improbable set of circumstances. Thirty minutes later I was back at camp wasting a cold can of beer and my partner was on a clean white bed at the hospital.

Not understanding fully what I had experienced and unable to describe it, I didn't attempt to explain to my companions. It was an entirely different world. Knowing the difference between not wanting to die and wanting to live, I began to look at people in a new way. For a while I could even tell when I met a person if he would know what I meant by "life." I felt this was more common among the Vietnamese than my GI buddies.

For this reason the operation described earlier is significant because for the first time I went on a combat operation knowing what life meant. The scenes described give an indication of the infinite little details that must be considered and how automatically most of them are done. More important, it offers an insight into the fine degree of efficiency to which men can be brought when training is directed to one specialty—how to kill. We were a well-trained team, with animal survival instincts and a reflex ability to kill and to know when not to kill. I had trained four of the men and two had been trained by another project member; Grady and I had probably been trained by the same instructors. We were the ultimate product of the machine: without orders or words, as if we shared a common brain, we knew what to do, when and how. We were disciplined soldiers, and as such we were able to be absolutely obedient to orders in the absence of orders. Obedience and a subconscious death-wish combined with well-honed survival instincts might serve to describe the ideal soldier.

On five occasions we had the choice of killing; on two we killed. We were the arbiters of life and death for other men; arbitrarily the decisions were made. In two of the cases there were many reasons for allowing the strangers to live, none of which had anything to do with right or wrong, justice, morality, democracy, freedom, liberty—or love. The decisions were made mechanically, pragmatically, and later I was deeply disturbed at how mechanically I continued to think—how intuitively— despite my new-found meaning for life. Ten years spent being trained to such a mechanical degree are not easily shucked. The man with the dinner pail will never know that his living was determined by whether he took a step to the side of the line he was walking; had he taken that step, any one of six unknown men would have dis- passionately slit his throat. By such things are life and death decided.

The process of changing a man into a soldier is brutal- izing even if he never kills another, and sadly, the indi- vidual seldom recognizes his own brutalization, his changing sense of values. The process of changing a nation into a military society is equally brutalizing, and just as sadly, few of its people recognize the transformation.

By allowing ourselves to become a military nation, we have forced much of the rest of the world to do so. I am not going to debate the chicken-and-egg question with regard to Russia. American and Russian militarists are undoubtedly interested in the same things—mili- tarists of all nations have more similarities than differ- ences, including distrust. A professional soldier moving from one army to another has little difficulty in adjusting —those in the French Foreign Legion are one example; those in our own army are another. But the fact is that our increased militarism has forced other countries to act accordingly and vice-versa. None, however, seems to have our propensity for using troops to settle political questions.

The more militaristic we become and force other nations to become, the more difficult it is to come to terms and the more frequent the stalemates. People who think continually in military terms, with their inherent values, distrust the motives of their counterparts in other countries; and forgetting that they are dealing with peoples, tend to think of negotiations as part of military maneuvers—a macabre chess game. The nuclear disarmament talks are a case in point. Time and time again last-minute excuses (some of them outright frauds) have precluded signing treaties. Not only is each side convinced that the other will use the treaty as a trap, but the military would feel forlorn if their finest toy were taken away.*

The people of Viet-Nam have been in a continuous state of war for over twenty years, which means that a third generation is growing up with guns in its hands and that their existence depends on their ability to think in military terms. Even if negotiations did not mean surrender of all or part of their sovereign rights, we could only expect the Vietnamese to be more intransigent and suspicious as the war progresses, not less.

A solution through negotiations which would involve the Vietnamese giving up something they have already won—in many cases twice—is complicated by the fact that it is a shooting war. It is one of those peculiarities of revolutionary wars that those who have lost the most and endured the worst privations are those least likely to

* In 1955 Russia agreed to nuclear disarmament, but we would only discuss control; in 1959 they even went so far as to allow on-site inspection. On both occasions we invented excuses to preclude agreement. They agreed to our terms and we backed out. (For additional information cf. daily newspapers of January 1959; *The Arms Race and the Case for Disarmament* by Phillip Noel-Baker; James Reston's Report on Secretary of Air Force Donald Quarles in *The New York Times*, September 1955; and *Congressional Record*, February 1960.)

stop fighting short of victory. It is unlikely that Americans can comprehend the soul-weariness and fatigue this war has caused in the South Vietnamese. For many there is no politics or nationalism—all that is left is a hate that can preclude "reasonableness." For the guerrilla, fighting has become a way of life, and before they are willing to give it up, they will want suitable compensation—which means the victory for which they have been fighting.

Future historians are sure to be puzzled by what we call an ideological conflict, for the differences between the great powers will be more difficult to discern than the similarities. Both camps, striving for economic power, are willing to use military power to attain it. One calls itself a "democratic republic," the other a "soviet republic"; neither name bears much resemblance to fact. Each points to its constitution as proof of its concern with justice and humanitarianism, and then overlooks it when that is more convenient. We fear almost irrationally the spread of socialism while living in a parasocialist society; the socialist countries retaliate against the spread of capitalism while building a paracapitalistic society. Pity the poor historian who must determine what we meant by communism—it could be Marx's theory of a socialist state or the government of the USSR; perhaps the Yugoslav or Chinese system or the one in the north of Viet-Nam? If it's the Russian system, do they choose the one of the thirties or the sixties? Will future historians ever figure out what a communist elephant or water buffalo is?

No less perplexing will be the task of deciphering "Free World." Does it mean the United States of America, where involuntary servitude for youth is the order of the day, where medals are given to the best killers and people are jailed because they don't wish to kill? Perhaps it means Spain or Portugal, but it could just as easily mean the south of Viet-Nam. Will it mean Australia, which supports the U.S.A., or France, which doesn't? If being non-communist is the criterion, then the Union of South Africa may be the model.

Will the future historian ever be able to understand why we regard communism as a monolithic evil seeking to take over the world, and simultaneously give aid to Poland, trade with Yugoslavia, and have cultural exchanges with Russia—while bombing Viet-Nam, a far lesser threat than the other three.

The hardest question to answer will be, Why, if we hate and fear communism, have we become the communists' major propaganda organ? Every time a people decides to fight for self-determination, we blame it on the communists; by continually giving the communists credit for all social changes in areas where the maintenance of the status quo is suicide, we build their prestige. Corrupt and dictatorial governments responsible for the conditions which breed revolts yell "Communists!" and on the theory that anything is better than communism, we rush to their aid. As a result fewer look to our government for guidance and more turn to the communists as their only source of help—and our propaganda once again becomes fact.

Most humanitarian actions in this country get the label—a movement to attain equality for Negroes is "communist-inspired"; the movement to stop the war is a "communist plot." It is ironic when Americans advocating peace are communists and those advocating war are good Americans—again the communists are given credit and are only too happy to take it.

Since fewer emerging countries look to us for guidance, nationalism is almost synonymous with communism and is, therefore, a thing to be prevented. This antagonism strangely increases as we progress closer to ultimate nationalism and absolute chauvinism. Is it possible that, unconsciously recognizing the threat of "*pox* americanus" to survival, we must prevent another from gaining equality, since two such nations would be catastrophic?

Communism is a threat because of our hysterical, irrational response to it and because we offer no viable alternative. Anything is justified in the name of anticommunism: witch hunts at home and CIA plots abroad. As a result of our actions in the past twenty years, the wonderful world we envisioned (modeled on American values) not only failed to materialize but is further away, and with rare exceptions our only "reliable" allies are governments we have created or bought.

The more desperately we fight blindly against communism, the less we understand what we are fighting. American students of Marxist theory and world politics have no qualms about talking or associating with communists; they have no fear of communism *per se* because they know and understand it. Student radicals find most of them outdated, too conservative, and generally dull, but because they have understanding without fear, they have no difficulty living alongside them or using their talents. It is a cause for great mirth when a demonstration is credited to the communists, since if it were really radical, they would have had to be convinced to participate. Those who know, know that we must fight neither drooling dragon nor voracious bear, but the fearful illusions that have formed the entire nation into a New Legion.

As a nation we have reached the point where we are interested in power for its own sake, much as a multimillionaire continues to amass new fortunes, even though he can't possibly spend what he has. For the nation it is an economic power backed by the military and its bases around the world. Yet we already own or control a disproportionate share of the world's wealth—and a nation that feels it can afford to spend sixty billion dollars annually on the military, down the tube, hardly needs additional sources of income. We don't need it; we just want it—if for no better reason than to show that we are right and "they" are wrong. This type of empire can be realized only through brute force or by the other nations' adoption of American ideals and ideology at the expense of their own aspirations and cultures.

In 1945 the world was overdue for drastic change, and in the following years people (if not their governments) were determined to end the status quo of contributing to their own impoverishment for the benefit of a few leaders and possibly a foreign country. During the same period the USSR was supposed to collapse under its own evil, instead of which it has refused to accept American policies and has made its presence felt over the world.

The primary motivation leading to our present state may have been economic, but in our striving for economic ascendancy we have developed an entirely new power and culture—militaristic bureaucracy. Organizations are created to perform a service, fill a need, achieve a goal; ostensibly in the interest of efficiency, bureaucracies are formed from within the organizational community to administer and direct it. The members of the bureaucracy soon develop a vested interest in keeping the organization alive, since only in this way can they maintain their position.

Once the need is fulfilled and the original goals met because of the services performed by the organization, it no longer has a function. Often, within organizations, original goals become confused, possibly because of a lack of communication (information hoarding). In either case the organization becomes meaningless, and motivation to join it disappears. When there is insufficient motivation to make the organization grow, it dies, and so does its bureaucracy. To keep the organization alive, the bureaucracy creates a crisis situation—an immediate need—to increase the motivation and inclination to join. Thus, the organization, created to perform a service required by outside interests, is now completely crisis-oriented and self-perpetuating.

Civilian control over the military was lost when World War II required that the military build a bureaucracy of unprecedented proportions with virtual control and use of the nation's manpower and wealth. In 1944, with the end of the war and of the large organization formed to win it in sight, plans were made to prevent the military's reversion to its lean prewar status.

Part of the military's arrogance is their belief that they can manage anything better than civilians. Having gained managerial power and liking its taste, the military were reluctant to relinquish it. They needed support, however, and turned to their wartime partners, industry. A more willing bedmate would be difficult to find: fat from war contracts and with the Depression a clear memory, the prospect of a permanent alliance was appealing. But the people had to be given some reason for maintaining, at their expense, a non-productive organization of such immensity. In 1945 only one other nation, because of its size and power, could seriously be thought of as a threat —Russia. The excuse for the machine would be the need for a peacetime draft.

Using millions of the people's money to bypass the Congress of the people, the military propagandists leaned hard on the panic button and literally bombarded the people with speeches, articles, editorials, movies, and exhibitions calculated to create a hysterical sense of crisis: the homeland was being threatened; the danger was imminent. With a helping hand from the Russian militarists in Berlin, the Pentagon had its way. It has become the world's richest organization (with three million men in uniform, a million civilians in its employ, and four million in defense industries, the military has the largest political bloc in the country, representing an enormous vested interest in the military state) * and the draft has been with us ever since.

The draft has not only provided bodies to flesh out the organization; it has guaranteed for the bureaucracy a never-ending succession of men capable of thinking militarily. Our conscription system gives the illusion of democracy, and much is made of the fact that our military is made up of "citizen soldiers"; what is overlooked is the corollary—soldier citizens. In socialist countries citizen soldiers are referred to as "peoples' armies."

The military bureaucrats spell out gloom and disaster at every opportunity—and how seriously the Pentagon believed its own propaganda is illustrated by the fact that when war broke out in Korea, there were only two hundred thousand men, many poorly trained, to put in the field, despite the five million personnel in Department of Defense. The solution to this crisis was not, of course, to reduce the top-heavy bureaucracy but to cry for addi-

* The Pentagon owns over thirty-four million acres of land; in Puerto Rico, for example, the U.S. military owns or controls over 15 percent of all arable land. For additional details, see Fred J. Cook, *The Warfare State* (New York: Crowell-Collier, 1962). In 1961, 86.4 percent of the $21 billion awarded to industry by the military involved no competitive bidding.

tional troops, which led in turn to an even larger bureaucracy.

Pundits, Politicians, Preachers, and Presidents know that the situation is wrong but their vested interest costs them the courage and patriotism necessary to take the steps to correct it. Yet our very survival depends upon reversing our military state. The Utopian situation would be complete elimination of the military; but nations have not yet reached the degree of sanity necessary to accept the idea that armies are not necessary if nobody has one. Meanwhile, the military must be removed from every facet of society and its role in the scheme of things must be reduced to the original one: to protect the people from attack by an outsider. Only then will we be able to strive for a vested interest in humanitarian progress instead of in a state of perpetual warfare.

The saddest aspect of our continuing and growing militarism is that in a world crying for change, we have become the proverbial pimple on the ass of progress—not only other nations' progress but perhaps even more so our own. We are offered capitalism as exemplified by the U.S.A. or socialism as practiced in Russia or China; yet none is adequate, viable, or acceptable. So preoccupied are the three countries with the others' military posture—and their own—that there is no inclination to seek alternatives; if such a search were successful it would go unrecognized, since whatever it might be would be incomprehensible to people who can think of national security only in terms of military might.

With so many people interested in maintaining the status quo, it is only natural that the government is, too; thus our two-party system has become a twin-party system. The myopic mentality directing us in 1945 has continued through four administrations and twenty-one

Congresses. The Presidency, supposed to represent all the people, has become increasingly preoccupied with its secondary function as Commander-in-Chief of the Armed Forces, and more often than not makes decisions on that basis. Every time it votes money for the military the Congress loses that much more control.

The military community must be kept out of politics and separated from society. Control and influence must be reversed so that society controls the military and its direct employees. While it is true that this huge bloc with a vested interest in perpetuating military thought and action are citizens like anyone else, the argument is invalid that taking away any of their rights would remove their desire to protect the country—that argument assumes a non-existent idealism. When the law was passed (in the Eisenhower Administration) making the military pay income tax, it was said that this would make them feel more American—thereby increasing their motivation to protect America; but the law also states that soldiers in a war zone (Viet-Nam) are exempt from paying income tax—to increase their motivation. If the military is so hung up on voting, let them start doing it in their own society—and we'll vote in ours.

The practice of giving civil service preference to ex-servicemen must be abolished, as should the corporate practice of hiring retired generals and colonels to act as lobbyists with their old comrades-in-arms for lucrative contracts. Congress must insist on an accurate accounting of all monies voted to the military to ensure that not one penny is used for PR campaigns—which includes abolishing the use by military units of resources and materials paid for through taxes to print propaganda pamphlets and leaflets in the name of training exercises. The military should no longer subsidize the movie industry by lending men and equipment for movies glorifying the military and warfare. In short, for our very survival, we must rid ourselves of militarism.

The worst social evil ever perpetrated on our country, the thing that makes it possible for militarism to flourish, must be destroyed—the draft. Only when the military is prevented from getting their hands on our young men in the first place will the American citizen stop thinking in military terms. The draft is not only the manpower pool, designed to perpetuate the military society, it is also the single most corrupting influence on young people today, even before it puts them through the military processing machinery. Rather than go to jail, young men docilely register for the draft, even though it violates their consciences, and then are "given" the option to apply as conscientious objectors. By allowing the military to rule on their consciences, they forfeit to it the right to define conscience and morality. By registering and then applying for CO status, the individual is saying, "The system is okay, but make *him* a killer, not me." A person conscientiously opposed to killing should not have to cooperate with a system designed to promote it. But because the military has set the ground rules for approval of a CO status, it often forces young men to lie to conform to the rules. Only the military has the ability to determine right and wrong; hence, saying that you would fight if the United States were invaded but will not fight in Viet-Nam because your conscience says it is morally wrong to be there, is grounds for rejection as a CO.

Other young men, not wishing to be drafted and unable to meet CO criteria, are encouraged to tell outrageous lies testifying to drug addiction, sexual perversion, physical handicaps, and psychoses of every description; others take active part in organizations on the Attorney General's subversive list—again, these men are saying, "Take him, not me." Others who love their country too much to contribute further to its demise are forced to seek sanctuary in places like Canada and are labeled cowards.

Others, in the colleges and universities, seek student deferment, which helps pervert the very purpose of those institutions, since the student is striving not for academic excellence but for grades. This leads to a tendency to accept instead of question and investigate; the dialogue so essential to learning is subverted and new ideas die at birth. The latest innovation is for the students to fight against each other in periodic deferment examinations to see who can stay and who will have to go and kill or be killed, instead of fighting the system imposing such a corruption of the campus. (This is a subtle refinement of the Nazi practice in Poland of registering the Jews and letting them fight among themselves to see who would be the first to go to the ovens.) * In college many find themselves enrolled in mandatory ROTC (Reserve Officers Training Corps), so even there they are not free of the military grasp.

Any number of businesses cooperate in this sickness by refusing to hire young men who have not "discharged their obligation." When they return from service, they will be working for people who have also been in the military. The cycle continues.

Since the Pentagon is the largest supporter of scien-

* Boys who cannot go to college because of scholastic or financial limitations are denied even this dubious choice, and they go through the mill while their contemporaries fight each other and more bitterness is created. Military recruiters go into the high schools and distribute their military-glorifying propaganda, many young men enlist (to get a choice) rather than wait to be taken at some unspecified time.

tific research, the student may end up at a university dependent for much of its income on the military. Thus, even the university has a vested interest in the military society, and as a result the humanities courses more often than not are designed to apologize for and make acceptable our way of life instead of challenging and improving it. Faced with the draft after school, many go into the science fields to improve the possibility of working on defense contracts in order to prolong deferment; others take "snap" courses to keep up their grades.

Many young men go from high school to four years of college and then into graduate school without a break; depending on their field of study, they reach their mid-twenties having seen little of the world except from a classroom. Most of these years will have been spent in bucking for grades, not in getting an education. They may survive without any severe neuroses but can they relate their books to the world off campus? So long out of the habit of questioning, assuming they ever had it, can they really contribute to a better society or will they become additional legions to support the status quo? Many have taken courses they don't want; many would like to take a break from time to time and walk around and look at the world—but they don't dare.

There is much talk about the draft, but most of it simply questions its equitability, not its validity in our society. One of the sadder aspects of the draft is that because it has been with us for so long, there is little conscious objection to it now. Considering the pressures of our military society on our young men, it is amazing that so many resist it and for such good reasons. How many of their parents would risk five years' imprisonment for an ideal? There are those who advocate a two-year involuntary servitude for boys and girls as soon as they leave school, anywhere between the ages of sixteen and thirty-four; surely there must be a better solution to the employment problem.

Not satisfied with what they have already done, the military, hoping to get young men for training before they have the chance to build up resistance to indoctrination, now want to concentrate on the eighteen-to-nineteen-year-olds. They also want to draft men rejected for education reasons and educate them in the military— which is really getting people to mold as desired.

The educating of large segments of the population in and by the military presents a danger difficult to overstate. When this educating is aimed at those least able to evaluate and question, the danger is multiplied. Cadets enter the Military Academy at West Point as teen-agers; they graduate as young adults with a bachelor's degree and a commission to the rank of second lieutenant. The cost to the military for each graduate is $50,000. Considering the product, it is not difficult to understand why the military considers the price a bargain. The attitude of the graduating class of 1966 illustrates the point: so many of the 579 graduates volunteered for Viet-Nam as their first tour of duty, that a selection system based on class standings had to be devised. The comments of one of the "lucky" 98 selected offer an insight into the military necessity of Viet-Nam and why the West Point graduates wanted to go there:

Cadet Lieutenant Philip D. Riley of Dedham, Mass., saw the Viet-Nam war as providing career Army officers "with a chance to keep up with the changing methods of warfare. . . . As an Army officer trained to fight, I feel we need this conflict in order to learn what we may face later." *

If we desire our eighteen- and nineteen-year-olds to continue their education, then the facilities should be made available within the civilian community—minus the pressures imposed by the draft system—so they will be free to choose, question, and evaluate. If the "rejects" are trainable and we can afford the manpower and money to train them, then they should be trained in other than military schools and in something more useful than how to kill efficiently . . . something productive and creative.

Equally bad is the Peace Time (*sic*) GI Bill, which provides tuition assistance *after* military service; in other words, there are those who are deprived of assistance because they have not accepted military life. If tuition assistance is necessary and advisable, and the monies for it are available, it should be given on a non-discriminatory basis and not controlled by the Department of Veterans Affairs.

If young men will seek higher education only because of the threat of conscription, we should look at what higher education is offering. If we can get people to defend our country from danger only through conscription, we had better look at our country and our definition of danger. Economics may be the axle around which the treadmill of our society revolves, but the draft is the beast that keeps it turning. If we don't get rid of it, the legions of this country will march forward into oblivion.

* *San Francisco Chronicle,* June 8, 1966.

ALTHOUGH THE VIETNAMESE would appreciate an American withdrawal from Viet-Nam, nothing would be accomplished if it only created a bloody crisis somewhere else. Although there are many places in our own hemisphere to choose from, the basic problem remains. We have proven the saying that you can't keep someone pinned down without staying down yourself: so preoccupied have we become with "our" picture of the world and its evils that we have been unwilling or unable to recognize the faults in our own society. As a consequence, fewer and fewer people look to us for guidance.

That some nations seek help and guidance from communism rather than our system should give us reason to examine what we are—not what we think we are. If we believe communism is wrong, we should be developing an alternative to it. That other nations do not choose to emulate us should indicate that Americanism, anti-communism, is not an alternative. Why should we export our society's imperfections or impose them on others? Instead of devoting our energies to anti-communism, we should be forging new ideas, building responsiveness to our own future.

We are all for self-determination for other nations—so long as they are willing to integrate into the U.S.

economic system; we have taken the position that those not wishing to Americanize are anti-American. We give millions of dollars in aid to other countries and call ourselves generous—when in fact we give it to eliminate communist influence and hope that it will prevent significant change. All we ask for our money is love, allegiance, and trade; sometimes our money can buy governments, but seldom people and never love. We give aid and arms to non-aligned governments—and then tell them how to spend and against whom the arms can be used, creating an aligned government and more world tension. Being given money does not necessarily destroy a people's pride —but accepting it after having been told they aren't capable of independent decision certainly does. We give aid to a country so it can achieve self-determination— but if it looks like "our man in ——" will not win, the CIA is put to work or other pressures applied. When people start agitating for change, we try to help by aiding the government—thus repressing the dissent instead of introducing the reforms. When we give this type of aid, we automatically take sides, usually against the people —little wonder that reformists must look for help elsewhere.

If we could destroy our paranoia about communism and start changing our conception of ourselves and the world, we could turn our attention to revolutionizing our own society. Before people will look to us for help and inspiration we will have to prove that we have a system that can sustain itself without establishing an economic empire to the detriment of others. When we are free to find ways to change ourselves, the socialist countries should do the same.

For too long we have mistaken wealth for progress. When we can demonstrate that our way encourages the world to strive for *their* ways, we can become a force for change. When we have something to offer as a model, we can think of helping others by encouraging them— not by putting down revolutions. Right now the best way we can help other people is not to take sides, and if we must give aid, it should not be given directly but dispensed by an international agency not beholden to the United States, one that will make sure it gets to the people and is not used to bolster a bureaucracy.

When we become a country representing continuing change and progress, we can help necessary revolutions to succeed before they become bloody conflicts. Instead of being known and feared for our legions, we should be a nation interested in helping peoples—not governments. We can if we have the courage.

EPILOGUE

I HAD ORIGINALLY INTENDED to include in this book possible solutions to the war in Viet-Nam. But events of the past twelve months have convinced me of the futility of advancing such plans, since our government is well aware of all the solutions; that none have been implemented proves only that there is no desire to do so. It is becoming more apparent that our greatest concern is that something will end the war in Viet-Nam before a military victory can be achieved (making Viet-Nam two countries in fact). Those who don't think along these lines are those who want it to last long enough to provoke a direct confrontation with China. As long as we insist on thinking of Viet-Nam as two countries, then bombing the North because it aids the fight against the Saigon-U.S. regime makes sense—militarily. Using the same military logic it makes good sense to bomb China and Russia—now.

It must be obvious to the reader that my impression of the Vietnamese people took a drastic change from the one held by most of my contemporaries. Before I left Viet-Nam, I was invited into many homes; I was even adopted by a family and known as "my brother"—this family was not supporting the NLF, but they had little love for the Saigon government. There were those who sincerely liked many Americans even thought they admitted it wasn't the rule; but even among these there was resentment of the overwhelming presence of U.S. troops on their land. Those who had an understanding of communism seemed to have no desire to exchange one imperfection for another; but as one refugee father put it, "We can live, if we must, under communism. But we die under the bombs."

I have not chronicled examples of Viet Cong terrorist acts; they exist, and in great number, but terror is an integral part of guerrilla warfare and they fight with what they have. However, as applied by the Viet Cong, it is a terror the people can understand—although cruel, it is more selective than saturation bombings. Can you imagine the terror of waking up in the middle of the night to a nightmare world of flying metal and rivers of flaming napalm? Blowing up GI billets and shelling Pleiku cannot be thought of as terror in the military sense, since they are military targets. Since incidences of enemy terror are readily released to the American public, there is no point in my rewriting them. Much as I feel for the Vietnamese people, I am concerned with our morality, not theirs. Left to themselves, the Vietnamese are quite capable of settling their own moral problems.

It was neither by accident nor oversight that I refrained from quoting or referring to such mammoth works as *The Professional Soldier* by Morris Janowitz, *The History of Militarism* by Arthur Vagts, and *The American Soldier* by Samuel A. Stouffer. I am not writing for those who would have the time or ability to evaluate such encyclopedias of militarism. Too often, such books are based only on information made available by the military for studies financed by the military. Studies of this sort tend to support a desired conclusion. (In Stouffer's case this was almost entirely true; this does not mean that his findings are incorrect, but I would have been much more impressed had the War Department given him the classified as well as declassified reports made at taxpayers' expense. Kinkead came to all the wrong conclusions for all the right reasons in *In Every War But One*.) Finally, I tend to be suspicious of professional sociological studies, since they are made not in the interests of science or society, but rather to learn how to manipulate both.

One last word on the subject of terror (I'm at a loss to understand how wars are possible without it). Since it is incomprehensible to our militarists that anyone would voluntarily support the NLF, they have constantly maintained that the Vietnamese give aid and support to the NLF only because of the application of terror. If the Vietnamese can be controlled through terror, why didn't it work for Ngo Dinh Diem? If Diem had to tie down most of his troops to control the people through terror, why doesn't the NLF have to? Assuming that the military explanation is true, now that they claim the people are cooperating with us we must assume that the terror of search-and-clear tactics preceded by artillery, napalm, and anti-personnel bombings are worse than the NLF's tactics. "Terror," as any student of guerrilla warfare will testify, is a technique of violent revolution having political direction and is preceded by political preliminaries so the people will understand it. Because of the political direction and the preparation, the Vietnamese is more capable of understanding the bombing of a bar or restaurant in Saigon than he is the indiscriminate destruction of whole villages by a non-political B-52.

I continually hear the complaint that the American public is not being told the facts about Viet-Nam. I disagree. More has been written and filmed about Viet-Nam than any war in history. Unfortunately, the number of people who will take the time to distinguish between fact and propaganda is steadily diminishing—I refer to those both for and against our involvement in Viet-Nam. We see in the newspapers what we want to see, and while there is some slanted reporting, many journalists, at great personal risk, try to report objectively what they see. Some reporters have a self-imposed censorship, but nothing to compare to that of the reader.

A person determined to become a theological expert would read the Bible, but his education would be sadly lacking if he read no further. The person who restricts his reading about Viet-Nam to a particular newspaper or journal because he likes its interpretation is guilty of censorship, whether his choice is *Time* or *I. F. Stone's Weekly*. Pure objectivity is always impossible; concerning Viet-Nam it is less likely because of the subject's emotional nature. Traveling with combat units months on end and seeing death all around is a poor way to retain objectivity—for the soldier's chances for survival depend in large part on his ignorance of the facts, and faced with the truth about Viet-Nam, he will not see it because he doesn't want to see it. In addition we are being daily deprived of our ability to judge truth. What are we to think when an organization like the Roman Catholic Church in this country can support our actions in Viet-Nam, and piously say, ". . . we must clearly protest whenever there is a danger that the conflict will be escalated

beyond morally acceptable limits . . ."? * While preach-
ing peace and brotherhood, the Bishops of Christ are
saying that the horrors of Viet-Nam are within "morally
acceptable limits." Where are these limits?

●　　●　　●

I feel no personal bitterness toward the Army or Special Forces. Throughout my service I was satisfied with
the progress of my career and took great pride in my
military abilities. I am not condemning the U.S. military
as the source of all evils—the military is exactly what
we have allowed it to become because of our fears, hates,
and prejudices. Many will think I have written for the
purpose of destroying Special Forces *per se*—some personal vendetta. I'll leave such things to Robin Moore.

Rather, I feel the need for a hard look at how we
utilize such forces. Special Forces helps illustrate that
this is not a world of good guys and bad guys. We pile
invective on our enemies for the things we say they do,
but we have no qualms about doing the same things,
given the same circumstances. As those who have been
or are still in Special Forces can verify, I could have
used much more devastating material if I were interested
in hatchet jobs. Although far short of their PR image,
Special Forces has attracted many exceptional men, and
the mystique is still such that even the worst rise above
their normal capacity once the beret is donned. Not only
would I enjoy talking to many of my former friends in
the Army, I think it would prove beneficial.

●　　●　　●

* *San Francisco Chronicle*, November 22, 1966.

Donald Duncan

On the day he died in an accident Richard Fariña said to me, "We communicate easily because we have lived by and with violence and have not let it destroy us or our thinking. Violence is death and death is the enemy because it takes away life."

About the Author

Born in Toronto in 1930, Donald Duncan—an American citizen—worked as an office clerk, lumberjack, foundry worker, and tree topper before being drafted into the U.S. Army in December, 1954. Mr. Duncan served in Germany and the United States as a squad and section chief in a self-propelled weapons unit and as a non-commissioned officer in operations and intelligence. In early 1961 he transferred to Special Forces, where his primary specialty continued to be operations and intelligence, although he was also trained in weapons, demolition, and communication. Mr. Duncan was sent to Vietnam in 1964 where he was assigned to Project Delta and also formulated tactics for operations in War Zone D and the An Lao Valley. He has been decorated with the U.S. Army Air Medal, and twice with the Bronze Star and the Vietnamese Silver Star. Recommended for the U.S. Silver Star, the Legion of Merit, and a battlefield commission, he instead resigned from the Army in late 1965. Upon his return to this country he spoke out strongly against U.S. Vietnam policy and published an article on this subject in *Ramparts* which brought him national attention. Currently military editor of *Ramparts*, Mr. Duncan is married and lives in Berkeley.